The
Urgency
of Preaching

KYLE HASELDEN

The
Urgency
of Preaching

HARPER & ROW, PUBLISHERS

NEW YORK, EVANSTON, AND LONDON

FIRST EDITION

D—N

LIBRARY OF CONGRESS CATALOG CARD NUMBER: *63–10751*

To Hase and Berry

Contents

Preface

Thirty years ago one of this country's most captivating preachers, addressing a group of ministers at a convention in Washington, D.C., astonished his listeners with a dramatic "Morituri te salutamus!" He predicted an early end for all pulpit ministries because he was convinced that radio preaching, just then reaching toward the zenith of its popularity, would put the ordinary pulpit out of business. A few great preachers, broadcasting from the great centers of communication, would in his opinion soon capture the nation's ears on Sunday mornings and empty the churches. It was a false prophecy based upon a faulty premise; radio preaching prospered but the churches also prospered.

Nevertheless, the prophecy did not miss the mark entirely. Subsequently there *was* a death in the pulpit. For one thing the kind of preaching represented by this prophet—sensational, startling, dramatic—died; one is hard put to name a single example of that kind of preaching today. Moreover, in these thirty years the number of scholarly American preachers with a nationwide, interdenominational reputation has dropped from twenty or more to an indifferent number. And, what is much more tragic, in the average parish the will to preach—the joy, enthusiasm, and urgency of preaching—diminished in our generation until preaching became a monotonous and dreaded routine for some ministers and a weekly ordeal for others.

This study, which touches only one of the many questions about the decline of the pulpit, asks what has happened to dissipate the urgency of preaching. I am not interested in reviving either popular or so-called great preaching but I am concerned that the eagerness to preach which once characterized the American pulpit be recaptured. We must discover therefore what has happened to the earnestness and the zeal of the Christian proclamation. In the beginning this inquiry deals with a secondary but nevertheless important matter: the minister's loss of confidence in the power of his principal instrument, the spoken word. The search then turns in Chapters 2 and 3 to the minister's loss of confidence in the urgency of the gospel. Along the way there is suggested to the reader that internal and indispensable sermonic design which determines by its presence or absence whether the sermon is effective or inadequate, biblical or secular. It is this internal pattern, rather than the sermon's literary or rhetorical quality or its homiletical perfection or the fact that it begins with a biblical text and ends with a Christian prayer, which is the criterion of the good sermon. Finally, in the search for a mood of eagerness, earnestness, and compulsion for our preaching we examine the minister's loss of confidence in himself. In reverse order we are asking what the minister thinks of himself, his message, and his instrument, how these thoughts sap vitality from his preaching, and what must occur if he is to find the joy and fulfill the duty of one called to preach.

The substance of this book was delivered as the John M. English Lectures on preaching at Andover Newton Theological School. For the privilege of giving these annual lectures in the fall of 1962 I am indebted to President Herbert Gezork and Dean Roy Pearson. One of these chapters was in part presented as the convocation address at the Oberlin College Graduate School of Theology on the invitation of Dean Roger Hazelton. Portions of these lectures appeared from time to time as editorials in *The Pulpit* and are used by permission of the Christian Century Foundation. I am indebted to Marjorie Brown, copy editor of *The Pulpit*, who typed the manuscript and who patiently endured repeated readings of some of these pages.

KYLE HASELDEN

The
Urgency
of Preaching

1

The Priority of the Spoken Word

It is an odd but well-known fact that one of England's greatest nineteenth-century preachers, Frederick W. Robertson, had a morbid contempt for preaching. This is the man from whose fountain, as Harry Emerson Fosdick once put it, many young preachers of a later day primed their pumps. Yet Robertson of Brighton—as this master of terse, lucid exposition came to be known—wrote to a friend, "I wish I did not hate preaching so much, but the degradation of being a Brighton preacher is almost intolerable. . . . Nor am I speaking of the ministerial office; but only the 'stump orator' portion of it—and that I cannot but hold to be thoroughly despicable."[1]

This distaste for preaching, repeatedly expressed in Robertson's letters, was deeply rooted in his moody, complex character. A delicate, sensitive nature coupled to a resolute will recoiled from the praise which was lavished upon him in fashionable Brighton even more than from criticism by his enemies. To Robertson such popularity was a vulgar insult to self-respect, the galling exposure of a life which preferred solitude and contemplation. But beyond his hypersensitive temperament and his extreme delicacy there was another reason for his scorn of preaching. Put bluntly, Robertson distrusted the pulpit. Preferring spiritual work to secular he nevertheless doubted the power of the pulpit to accomplish spiritual ends. He concluded, perhaps erroneously, that the people's praise was for the charming style rather than the skillfully worked substance of his preaching and consequently he lost confidence in the power of preaching. Near the close of his brief ministry—he died at age thirty-seven—he wrote of the pulpit, "How slight the power seems to me to be given by it of winning souls."[2]

However, what Robertson was lamenting over a hundred years ago was something more than the ineffectiveness of the pulpit in winning souls. He mourned the decline of the preacher as the soul of civilization. Perhaps more correctly, he regretted the disappearance of the parson as the representative member of society. Here we see in Robertson the restrained pride which often underlies fine-honed sensitivity. In words that reveal that pride as well as his regret he wrote of the pulpit, "By the change of times the pulpit has lost its place. It does only part of that whole which used to be done by it alone. Once it was newspaper, schoolmaster, theological treatise, a stimulant to good works, historical lecture, metaphysics, etc., all in one. Now these are portioned out to different officers, and the pulpit is no more the pulpit of three centuries back. . . ."[3] He visualized the pulpit as the prow of civilization and wanted it to be what Herman Melville called it in *Moby Dick,* "this earth's foremost part." Despite the beauty of his personality he lacked that quality of character which made William Carey say about his son who left the mission field for government service, "My son Felix has shrivelled from a missionary to an ambassador."

Press this analysis and one is forced to the conclusion that Robertson did not see in the preaching of the gospel and in that alone a sufficient justification for the existence of the pulpit. If the pulpit as in former times could have been many things to many men, he would have thought well of it; but despite the keenness of his spiritual sensitivity—or because of it—he could not think highly of a pulpit which had dwindled from many roles to one. Thus Robertson, detecting a century ago what an eroding stream of time and culture had done and would do to the preaching province of the ministry, raises for us questions about the necessity for, and the efficacy of, preaching. Now that preaching has been almost completely stripped of the multiple authorities after which Robertson hankered and has only one authority left—and that not its own— has its usefulness passed? Now that the scope of preaching has been reduced to the proclamation and the teaching of the gospel of Jesus Christ, is it necessary? Since the preacher, as P. T. Forsyth said much later, can no longer beard kings, bend senates, determine policies, rule fashions, and prescribe thought, must the role of the clergy shrink still further until there is nothing left of it but the pastor and the priest? Is the preacher an anachronism? Is preaching a kind of ecclesiastical reflex action which lingers long past its usefulness and drains off energies which could be better used elsewhere?

Such questions, as Robertson and Forsyth demonstrate, are not new. Indeed, even the Apostle Paul had something to say about "the foolishness of preaching." What is new is the mood in which such questions are raised today and the effect of that mood upon the preached word. In the past men expressed the same doubts about preaching that we express, but they continued to give preeminence to preaching. They knew the questions but they also had answers which we seem to lack. They expressed their doubts about preaching with twinges of regret; we raise ours with ease, sometimes with delight. They saw no alternatives to preaching; we think we see many. They were suspicious of preaching but preached great sermons; we flinch when the word *great* is linked to the word *sermon*.

Indeed, there is in this country a school of homiletics which seems dedicated to stamping out any preaching except that which throws the whole burden on the Holy Spirit. It is a kind of antinomianism which holds that the poorer one preaches the greater the opening for the Holy Spirit. Lay on the handicaps and give God the glory! As though preaching were two separate and distinct things—what man does and what God does—rather than one thing—what God does when he selects, ordains, empowers, and employs the preaching powers of his servant.

Robertson had his doubts about preaching but what he preached made news. What we preach seems not to matter. When the writer became the editor of *The Pulpit* in the early months of 1960 he initiated a little column called "Sermons in the News." Three months later he had to abandon this novelty, not because he had no access to the nation's best preaching but simply because there was a paucity of newsworthy sermons. (The spate of impassioned sermons which greeted the Supreme Court decision on the New York State Regent's prayer seems to contradict this dismissal of sermons as not newsworthy. The decision did summon from us many good sermons—and some bad ones. But note that the decision made sermons; sermons did not make the decision.) Say what we will about the general level of preaching in this country being higher than it has ever been before—which may be true but is hard to prove—we have to grant that the general level is still low and that there are today no preachers who have a nationwide reputation and influence comparable to the kind wielded in the past. As someone said recently about the nation's economy, preaching is stagnating on a high plateau.

It may be that preaching is actually in a valley between two plateaus, one gone and the other yet to come, or it may be that the great ages of preaching have gone forever. The editor of *The*

Pulpit occasionally receives letters which ask, "Why don't you give us some great sermons in your journal of preaching?" Well, there *are* some. But instead of trying to point them out the editor is tempted to reply as Woodrow Wilson, when president of Princeton University, did to parents who asked, "Why don't you make more of our boys?" He answered, "Because they are your boys." But this would be arrogant; so the reply is a promise that if the critic will name the great preachers of our day, *The Pulpit* will secure sermons from them. So the critic sends his list: Fosdick, Scherer, Buttrick, Sockman—every one of whom was in his heyday a quarter of a century ago. *The Pulpit* is a journal of contemporary preaching and its efforts to discover the peers of such men in craftsmanship and in influence in the new generation have thus far been futile. Not to defend this journal but because it is the truth it must be said, "Because they are your boys." Whatever the explanation it is commonplace and correct to conclude that preaching is in the doldrums.

Do we care? The regretful conclusion is that we do not. We preach because preaching is expected of us; we preach well enough to get by; but we do not preach under the kind of compulsion which made Paul say, "For necessity is laid upon me. Woe to me if I do not preach the gospel!" (I Cor. 9:16b). We do not share the passion of Richard Baxter's "Preach as never sure to preach again and as a dying man to dying men." We do not mount our pulpits Sunday after Sunday with the awful feeling that under God's appointment we are dealing with men in terms of life and death and by God's grace are communicating to them eternal verities which reach beyond life and death. Our mood, in a word, is one largely untouched by the urgency of preaching.

To ask why this is so is to enter an area too vast for thorough exploration here. A complete analysis of the decline of preaching and the loss of a compelling urge to preach would probe the effect of the rise of the state and the paralleling displacement of the church as the people's authority. It would note the ascending prestige of scientists, statesmen, and psychiatrists as the revered and trusted priests of our age. Such a study could not ignore embarrassing statistics—such as those compiled by Mark A. Way—which show that there has been a long, downward trend in the intellectual capacity and educational status of the Christian ministry. To get the whole answer we would have to ask what effect the general mood of secularism and nativism has upon the clergy as an "amorphous religiosity" suffuses our Western culture. We might want to ask what is meant by the fact that the decline of the evangelical clergy in its preaching function was preceded by a diminishing of the popular use of the Bible. (Where does this vicious circle begin? How can it be broken?) We would have to measure the drawing power of radio, television, and motion pictures on the eyes and ears of men, in competition with the pulpit. We might even want to know whether the steady erasure of many traditional superstitions by science and popular education and the simultaneous shrinking of the pulpit's influence are anything more than coincidental parallels. Were great pulpits produced by the people's hunger for the occult, the mysterious, and the authoritative word and has that hunger now developed a new taste which the pulpit cannot satisfy? Moreover, what effect does the removal of churches from the nerve and tension centers of great cities to the antiseptic suburbs have upon preaching?

The questions are many. Preaching has been so long and so much a part of our culture that to study its decline is to send inquiries into almost every area of our common life. We must settle here for answers which are much more limited in their focus but which for that reason may be the ones most pertinent to our need.

The Apostle Paul's confession, "Woe to me if I do not preach the gospel," suggests two close-tied explanations of the waning power of preaching in these middle years of the twentieth century. These two explanations are unequal in value, but they are inseparable and we must consider both. We shall do so in an order which leads from the lesser to the greater.

First, then, the ebbing of the power and the compulsion of preaching is directly related to the clergy's loss of confidence in the power of the spoken word. In a day when more people than ever before in the history of language are using public speech with skill and effectiveness, ministers, whose chief tool is the spoken word, have in general less skill and less training in oral communication than men and women in a host of other professions. What a commentary it was on our profession when ministers in California, long in service, asked Charles Laughton, an actor and a superb one, to teach them how to read the Bible in public. This is an art which actors should learn from preachers. What a judgment it is when a guide in the Argonne Laboratories speaks with a precision, clarity, and charmingly modulated voice which puts to shame the touring ministers under his care; when television announcers and commentators show more respect for the artful possibilities of the human voice than do ministers who use the same oral capacities for a spiritual rather than a secular profession. We would not think of using an untrained mind to explain the scriptures, to interpret church history, to relate an eternal gospel to man's current need and condition. For that we are convinced that we need at least four years of college and three or four of seminary training under the ablest teachers we can secure. And we are right. But we assume that whatever kind of voice we have and whatever skills in expression are native to us are good enough to transmit such hard-earned knowledge and precious insight to our people.

We wince when we see a seminary's homiletics department so cluttered with electronic gadgets that there is no room for students. But our seminaries today rarely err on this side. On the contrary homiletics, being a practical study, a craftsmanship, is hidden away in most seminaries as though it were the black sheep of the theological family. Pity keeps us from turning it out into the cold, but we refer to it with shame. And homiletics in turn is embarrassed by any reference to the cultivation of the human voice and the perfection of its uses. There is obviously a vast difference in degree, but it is difficult to see any difference in principle between the training of the mind—which in the last analysis is also an instrument—and the cultivation of the vocal organ and the art of vocal expression. This may be debatable, but there is no denying the fact that there is a needless blockage and seepage of Christian knowledge and insight and a loss of persuading pressure when ministers in their preaching rely upon a vocal transmitter which has not been brought to its full power. This is not to say that a man has no place in the Christian pulpit until he becomes a little Cicero. Better a boorish stammerer with the gospel than a polished orator without it. But why do we have to choose between the two? It is to say that a minister who willfully uses in the gospel's service less than what he could use, who puts his "apples of gold" in battered crates when he could put them "in a setting of silver," is not only wasteful but is also sacrilegious.

How do we explain the clergy's loss of confidence in the spoken word? Perhaps it comes about because the clergy knows better than most men how cheap words are and how dangerous they can be in the mouths of mischievous men. The impersonal, mechanical perfection of the announcer who speaks with passion and finesse but may not believe a word he speaks; the cunning persuasiveness of the smooth-tongued, platform charlatan as he appeals to men's hatred and fear; the unfortunate experiences of some of our charismatic colleagues whose enticing powers in the pulpit have sometimes catapulted them into ruinous escapades in the parish; the deceit of little men who, in Ruskin's words, "play stage tricks with doctrines of life and death"; the ominous tirades of the Hitlers and the Mussolinis leading their people to their doom—we have had our fill in this day of glib words which are not worth the sound it takes to utter them, of enticing words which do evil rather than good, of terrible words which massacre whole races and plunge the world into disaster. We are rightly suspicious of the power of the spoken word.

Even so, we must not make Robertson's mistake. Suspecting that his "gift of gab" was drawing the wrong kind of response from the people and having the wrong effect upon them, this master of the spoken word began to distrust the power of the spoken word. But the evil that men do with their voices rather proves than disproves the power and the usefulness of the human voice. And the fact that such amoral power is widely used for an evil end should challenge us to use it for a good one. So, at least, Augustine reasoned in his *On Christian Doctrine*. He said, "For since by means of the art of rhetoric both truth and falsehood are urged, who would dare to say that truth should stand in the person of its defender unarmed against lying, so that they who wish to urge falsehoods may know how to make their listeners benevolent, or attentive, or docile in their presentation, while the defenders of truth are ignorant of that art? . . . While the faculty of eloquence, which is of great value in urging either evil or justice, is in itself indifferent, why should it not be obtained for the uses of the good in the service of truth if the evil usurp it for the winning of perverse and vain causes in defense of iniquity and error?"[4] Or, as we would put it, why turn over to the enemy the best weapon, the spoken word?

In the communication of the gospel the spoken word is the best weapon, the superlative tool; in this area it has superiority over all other forms of communication. Consider first the testimony of Paul. It does no violence to his apostrophe if we break it off bluntly and make Paul say—as he would have—"Woe to me if I do not preach. . . ." Pope John XXIII has somewhere said that if the Apostle Paul were living today he would be a journalist. The Pope has by this saying endeared himself to all journalists, who, of course, assume that the widest and quickest promulgation of an idea in our day is achieved by the printed word. Yet, knowing Paul, it is inconceivable that he would in any day surrender preaching in its traditional form, however much he might use other media of communication. He was constrained to preach: a necessity was laid upon him to deliver the gospel to men not only through their eyes in the reading of his letters but also in person through their ears in the hearing of his voice. With him preaching had priority over writing. Indeed it had priority over the administration of the sacraments. He wrote to the Corinthians, "For Christ did not send me to baptize but to preach the gospel" (I Cor. 1:17a).

Paul was writer and preacher. Perhaps we should say that he was a preacher who used whatever instrument was available. But there is every indication in his own word and deed that he would not have surrendered the best weapon of all, the spoken word. One bit of evidence will do where many could be submitted. He wrote as we know "to all God's beloved in Rome" such a letter as has never been seen before or since. Make a list of the greatest documents ever written, measured in terms of influence on human history, and you must put Paul's letter to the Romans near the top.

Repeatedly this letter has turned the church right side up again and has exploded a stagnant Christian theology into life, sometimes with broad and deep effect upon social, economic, and political as well as ecclesiastical history.

You would think that sending such a letter, so full of Christian insight that we in the church have barely begun to tap its riches, would have been enough even for Paul. But it was not enough. In that letter he said, "For I long to see you, that I may impart to you some spiritual gift to strengthen you, that is, that we may be mutually encouraged by each other's faith, both yours and mine" (Rom. 1:11-12). So, there are spiritual gifts which cannot be transferred by the written word or obtained by the writing of a letter. Thus it was that Paul, like a fretful pigeon locked in a foreign cage, yearning for home, was drawn irresistibly toward Rome. When every other effort failed to take him there, he courted death by appealing to Caesar and was on his way to Rome and to death. Why? Why all this bother and why the running of such a risk? He tells us why: "I am eager to preach the gospel to you also who are in Rome" (Rom. 1:15). A journalist? Probably. But he was a journalist who knew that the written word, powerful and beautiful though it may be, can never supplant the spoken. "Eager to preach. . . ." Almost anywhere you catch a picture of Paul in the New Testament, that could be its caption: before Jews and Gentiles, in jail and in the middle of the Areopagus, at sea and in shipwreck, to Agrippa and Bernice, at Ephesus and in Rome, he was eager to preach. He was ardent in proclaiming the gospel in any way he could, and later we must ask some questions about this ardor. But specifically he was eager to *preach* the gospel because he sensed as we do not the priority of the spoken word.

The superiority of speech over every other expressive act used in the propagation or celebration of the gospel does not mean that we must deride and discard all other media. Words, as important as they are, are not things; and sometimes the thing itself, too intimate or too indefinable for the word, will seek some other expression. God's Son was a preacher—"Jesus came preaching. . . ." But God's Word was given to us in an act. We ministers cannot repeat the act but we can bear witness to it. We use in that witness whatever instruments we can, but we must not neglect the one best suited to our purposes and the one for which we are best fitted. "Music hath charms. . . ." Agreed, but music does not have precision. The chorus of Beethoven's Ninth Symphony can be, as it was written, a non-Christian hymn to joy or it can be, as Henry van Dyke's words make it, an adoration of the Christian God. It depends upon the lyrics; the melody is indifferent and indefinite. A painting—take Rembrandt's "Christ at Emmaus"—can create in us in the first swift view a mood which leaves us wordless; but whoever says that one picture is worth a thousand words has never tried to put John 3:16—twenty-five words—into a picture.

A ritualistic act—removing the scroll from the ark, elevating the host, sharing the broken bread—can become a holy symbol for the people initiated into its use. But the meaning of the act is always dependent upon a preliminary or an accompanying word. Sermons can be put in tracts and mailed to shut-ins. But a printed sermon is a pressed flower: all of the color and the fragrance and some of the substance disappear. No sermon can ever be as good in print as it was in speech. Whatever we say about it, the gospel will and should seek expression in all these and in many other forms: in liquid music, immutable sculpture and painting, frozen architecture, dramatic ritual and timeless print. We preachers ought to rejoice in this fact rather than petulantly resent it, but we should not let it divert us from our appointment to the preached Word.

Nowadays it is faddish in the church to experiment with odd

forms of religious expression: film strips against a symphonic background, dial-a-prayer telephones, liturgical dances, jukeboxes in the church parlor. Is this a sign of health or a symptom of disease? It could be either. It could be that we are so full of so much to tell of the good news of Jesus Christ that it flows out in all directions, filling all vessels and spilling over into all channels. But it could also be that our current infatuation with the unusual, even the bizarre, in communication is a reflection in the church of an endemic sickness in society. Whichever it is we should at least be warned that the hunger for novelty, for some new thing, with a corresponding contempt for the old solely because it is old, is usually a mark of cultural adolescence or social degeneracy.

There is, of course, a third possibility which the older generation must not overlook. It may be that the new generation's contempt for the tools of the old is youth's impatient protest against the elders' ineffectiveness in the use of those tools. Perhaps the new generation is turning to unconventional media of communication not because it has a taste for the exotic but because it is desperately searching for an adequate substitute for the sermon, a substitute made necessary by the apparent ineptness and futility of preaching. This generation must discover for itself as others before it have that the only adequate substitute for poor preaching is good preaching. The word which the Apostle attached to preaching was *foolishness*, not *futility*.

In this connection it is amusing that the homiletical fashion which today scrupulously minimizes all literary craftsmanship in the preparation of the sermon, which insists that a sermon always be a simple, unstudied proclamation of the crucified and risen Christ—lest we deal in worldly wisdom and in enticing words rather than in the Word of God—is often the same one which is addicted to bizarre uses of religious language in other settings. This mode insists that the sermon be entirely artless and unadorned, that it be hurled at the congregation like a shapeless stone. Yet at the same time, spurning conventional proclamations of the gospel, this prevailing taste adopts media of proclamation which require the most artificial use and the most elaborate embellishment of the spoken word. So we have a vogue which runs to religious skits, illustrated talks, monologues superimposed on Mozart symphonies, speech choirs, nondirected discourses set against a jazz background, liturgical dances with appropriate cues for the spectators, and dialogue sermons. To be sure, there is no exclusive vessel for the transmitting of the gospel, and there is no medium of communication which alone is adequate for the fullness of the gospel. Experimentation is always in order. But the point is this: if every kind of artistic and artificial device can be brought to the aid of words and if words can be made to serve every other expressive device, why are the words of the sermon no longer privileged to unfold and employ their own potential powers? If every other kind of dramatic and artistic artifice can be put at the gospel's disposal, why must we deprive it of the powerful aid of literary ingenuity?

No one need fear that the florid style of pulpit oratory which flourished a hundred years ago and which has been dying out ever since will in our time return to the Christian pulpit. There may be an exception here and there, but that kind of rhetoric is gone and to cry alarm against it is to bark at a hollow log. As a matter of fact Beecher, Spurgeon, Chalmers, Brooks, and many of their contemporaries had already discovered in the mid-years of the nineteenth century the power of chaste, unadorned language.

The spoken word, we are saying, is an instrument especially suited to the promulgation of a gospel; it is the form into which an urgent message most naturally flows. For whatever tradition is worth, this was the experience of missions, prophecy, and evangelism throughout biblical history. When God would speak to men he sometimes chose a writer but much more frequently he chose a sayer: Amos, Jonah, Jeremiah, Ezekiel. In volume at least the Bible has a preference for "go, tell" over "write, send." It has a preference for the direct confrontation of speaker and hearer over the relaying of a message from scribe to reader. Let eye meet eye and word fall on ear.

But the argument for the spoken word as the preferred instrument of proclamation rests on something more than biblical tradition. Let a journalist, whose trade deals exclusively in the printed word, confess that the spoken language antedates the written. It does so in the history of the race. Anthropologists are disagreed, but many of them believe that there were meaningful animal cries in our throats even before there were attempts at gestural communication. At least we know that vocal expressions, the forming of cries and grunts into words, preceded by thousands of years written expression, the symbolizing of words in script. In its social if not in its intellectual beginning, the human race was born talking and listening. The written language has become much more than this in the modern era of abstract and technological thought, but at first it was merely a substitute for the vocal language. It met the requirements of distance and time as the audible word, ephemeral and limited in space, did not. But thousands, perhaps millions of years before we wrote to one another we talked and listened to one another. Whatever else it has become, human communication—the foundation of society—was originally vocal and therefore it was called a language; that is, a tongue, a speaking, and a hearing. This sociological fact has a deep psychological significance.

Moreover, even in this land of almost universal literacy, the spoken language antedates the written in the development of the individual. We call a baby an infant—combining two French words—because at birth it cannot speak. Yet how easily and quickly—viewed ex post facto—these speechless ones learn to talk. And, given the baby's natural mimetic ability, why not? From the day of its birth an incessant stream of vocal sounds falls upon the baby's ears. And in the process the one who speaks, the *other,* the one out there, becomes familiar and identifiable. The cry and coo of the baby and the responding or initiating voice of its mother create for the child its first experience of interpersonal communication. Not through the baby's eyes but through its ears its mother first becomes something more than a mass of warmth and nourishment. A mother who talks to her baby long before it understands imparts to her child the essential sounds of spiritual exchange and prepares the child for the primitive and prerequisite signals of human communion: *I, you, we.* As has been many times proved, this can happen to the deaf and the mute; but what a long, tedious process such learning is and how easily and quickly tongue and ear accomplish what eye and hand must labor to obtain.

The antiquity of speech in the racial and in the individual development, its success in each case in promoting the human affinity and the spiritual exchange, gives the faculty of speech a psychic as well as a practical excellence over all other forms of communication. The tongue's ability to put meaning and feeling into sound and the ear's ability to extract meaning and feeling from sound are learned rather than instinctive powers. But they were learned so long ago in our racial history and so deep in our childhood that they are only slightly removed from our animal instincts. In the beginning the voice was the organ of our visceral reactions: fear, alarm, hatred, hunger. It became consequently the organ of the soul's reactions: love, jealousy, hope, despair, courage, faith, aspiration. It is not surprising that the voice opens chambers of our being which the written word, however precise and powerful, cannot even touch.

It has been doing this for us and to us as a race since the dawn of human consciousness. It has been doing this for us and to us as individuals since our mothers' voices first whispered us awake to the possibilities of I and thou.

The more we think about the miracle and the mystery of the human voice, the articulated breath in our mouths, the more we are tempted to wax sentimental and to accept Longfellow's exaggeration: "The soul reveals itself in the voice only." We must not say "in the voice only." There is an art and a music and a literature and somewhere tied up in ribbons a bundle of letters which prevent our saying that the voice is the only organ of the soul. But we can say that the soul reveals itself in the voice more constantly, more practically, more intelligibly than through any other medium. Truly, "we preach not ourselves," not even our own souls, "but Jesus Christ as Lord." But we preachers are not commercial announcers reading whatever script we are paid to read whether we believe it and feel it or not. We are not wax records repeating, when the machine is started at 11:00 A.M. on Sundays, the sounds impressed upon us externally. The sermon rises out of our interior parts. We are living souls seeking direct communication with living souls, bearing personal testimony not to our truth but to a revealed truth which, received, we believe and feel. For this we have many instruments but none superior to the spoken word. Said the ancient wise man, "Death and life are in the power of the tongue, and those who love it will eat its fruits" (Prov. 18:21). The power of the spoken word is not debatable. We who are ordained as ambassadors of life and of *the* Life must not surrender the power of the tongue to the agents of death.

2

The Urgency of Preaching

The Apostle wrote, "Woe to me if I do not preach the Gospel." To stress the importance of the spoken word we took some permissible liberties with that saying, but we must avoid the errors into which those liberties could lead us. When Paul wrote this line to the Corinthians there was no pause between the word *preach* and the words *the gospel*. He knew no urge to be an orator even though he lived in a day when eloquence was revered. He seized the most effective medium—preaching—because he was constrained to transmit the most important message—the gospel. However great the inherent power of the spoken word, it received in his mouth a greater power as the instrument of a gospel which demanded declaration. There is really only one way to sketch the profile of the Apostle after he had traveled the Damascus road: he was a possessed man. In his preaching as in everything else he was under orders he could not disobey. Those orders included the preaching of the gospel.

It is this mood which drove and drew the Apostle all over the Mediterranean basin, loosing his tongue in strange places, proclaiming through the foolishness of preaching an "absurd" gospel about an "absurd" cross. And this mood, now so infrequent in our preaching, marks every so-called great sermon produced by the church, from Peter's sermon to the rulers, elders, and scribes gathered in Jerusalem to George A. Buttrick's "Lonely Voyage" preached to faculty and students at Harvard University. Old as they are such sermons as Chrysostom's "Excessive Grief at the Death of Friends," Augustine's "The Recovery of Sight to the Blind," Luther's "The Method and Fruits of Justification," and Bunyan's "The Barren Fig Tree" still grip us with their pressure and insistence even in written form. There is in such sermons a kind of radioactive earnestness which does not diminish with the passage of time. They are time- less because they were timely: they pressed upon the hour with intense earnestness, immediacy, and demand.

This is the reason why the rescue of preaching in our time de- pends primarily upon our being recaptured by the passion of the whole gospel and only secondarily upon a renewed respect for the power of the spoken word. All of us recognize the fact that con- temporary religious thought is hampered by threadbare words, by an accumulation of unintelligible theological jargon, and by stale, flat sermonic language. The Third Assembly of the World Council of Churches was expressing our discontent when it issued a call for a renewal of theological language. The old words have lost meaning and impact; the new words are artificial and esoteric. Therefore, the Assembly stressed the "urgent need for a radical revision of theological language so that it can be made intelligible to contemporary people throughout the world." Few people would refute the fact that the vocabularies of theologians (including the most important theologians of all—the parish ministers) need to be renewed and refurbished.

But the Assembly's enticing suggestion raises a question: How can we achieve a radically revised or a new theological language? Languages are not produced by fiat; they are never the result of scientific projects; they cannot be arbitrarily manufactured. Vast effort and abundant erudition have been invested for a long period of time in the attempt to produce a universal language, but thus far the returns have been meager. Who remembers Ido, Ro, and Volapuk, all of which were attempts in the past one hundred years to create a universal tongue? But while such attempts failed, the wild growth of idioms and dialects flourished and the virile sciences of our time had no deficiency of apt and precise terms. The name comes with the baby.

This contrast between the failure of contrived languages and the success of artless dialects and scientific terminology suggests that necessity is the mother of language as it is the mother of every other invention. It suggests further that the necessity which produces a new language has to be something more than dissatisfaction with an old language. Put it this way: as molten, volcanic lava carves out its own path and paves its own way, so new, intense, vital human experiences create their own verbal vehicles. Or, like seeds which grow their own shells about them, new ideas, new feelings, and new relationships produce their own literary containers. Language is a product of the compulsions of human experience —the joys need to sing, the pains need to cry, the sorrows need to sob, the ideas need to be remembered and transmitted, the loves need to be known, the prayers need to be uttered.

First the experience, then the word to fit it. First the reality, then the definition. So it was in the beginning: first the creation and then God gave names to his creations: night, day, sun, and moon. First the creation and then God brought all living things before the first man and the first man gave every living thing its name. There was no dearth of names, no shortage of language, so long as there was no lack of living things.

This fact does not eliminate the need for literary craftsmanship. What Adam named Aristotle had to classify; what we feel as keenly as Shakespeare, Shakespeare will say better and help us say better. But whenever the human experience, good or bad, is real, is vital, it will create its own tongue. And where there is no real experience, all the linguistic experts in the world cannot generate experience and reality merely by fabricating a new language or by revising an old one. What is true of the colloquialisms which rise out of the soil of common experience is true also of the language of religion. Either the new theological language will be lived into being, will be produced in agony and aspiration as men seek and receive the will and the power of God for them in their time, or the new theological language will be artificial and useless.

Words fail us, we sometimes say, and sometimes they do. The experience comes with such suddenness or such power that we are silenced by it. But more often *we* fail words. Like the frequently referred to little boy who did not speak until he was five years old, we are silent not because we do not know the words but because we have nothing to say, because there is nothing in us which demands declaration. So, if first the sickliness of preaching comes from our lack of confidence in the spoken word, then, second, the waning of the power and the effectiveness of our preaching is directly related to our lost sense of the urgency of the gospel.

Why, for example, is there such a dearth in our day of what we sometimes call prophetic preaching? Why is so much of our preaching tangential to the real issues of real lives in a real world? Why are there in it few of God's judgmental and redemptive words for the arenas in which men struggle: race, politics, war, and the socially accepted antisocial practices? To say that we ministers lack courage is to offer a partially true but fundamentally inadequate answer. There is truth in it: the comforts, prestige, and adequate salary of a "good" church; the financial strains of a daughter in college and the payments on the new car coming up with harassing regularity; the ubiquitous eye of a bishop or a pastoral committee ever on us—such things make moderates of us all.

Nevertheless, ministers falter in their prophetic role not primarily from a lack of courage but fundamentally from a lack of conviction. Courage, in human beings, is quite a different thing from what is called courage in the gamecock or the bull or the bulldog. In them bravery, if we can call it that, is a built-in, self-generating quality. It is instinctive; specifically, it is not bravery but recklessness. The thought of flight, of cautious withdrawal, never occurs to such creatures. But it does occur to a man. And when a man, threatened at the very center of his being, stands in the presence of danger he acts on the basis of something antecedent to courage.

If this is true of ordinary human courage it is even more so of Christian courage. Christian courage requires not so much that a man be brave as it does that he be borne. He does not stand his ground—his ground stands him. It holds him up and it holds him fast. Christian courage is Martin Luther saying—not with grim, proud, stoical resolution or Hollywoodish braggadocio but with surrender to God—"Here stand I; God help me; I can do no other." He meant just that; he did what he did because under God he could not do otherwise. You can use his "Here stand I" as a declaration of religious freedom only if you add his "God help me; I can do no other" as a confession of spiritual bondage. Christian courage is Robertson of Brighton's reply to a woman who assailed him for his heterodox views, warning him of dire consequences in this world and the next. To her surprise he said, "I don't care." And when she retorted, "Do you know what 'don't care' came to, Sir?" he answered, "Yes, Madam, he was crucified on Calvary."[1] Christian courage says "I don't care" to one set of values and dangers because about other values and other dangers it cares supremely. Christian courage is Paul in his letter to the Philippians veering sharply upward from a stoic's language about the true, the honorable, the just, the pure, to a Christian's vocabulary about utter dependence upon God through Jesus Christ: "I can do all things in him who strengthens me." Christian courage is not the summoning of some internal, natural force equal to the worst assaults of life; it is obedience to Jesus Christ and reliance upon his power.

Pushed still further, Christian courage is produced in us not because we are committed to Christ and cannot let our hero down but because Christ is committed to us—"For their sake I consecrate myself, that they also may be consecrated in truth" (John 17:19)—and he will not leave us desolate. Christian courage is wholly derivative. It is Jesus Christ in us. And if he is not in us, there may be a boldness and bluff in our preaching, there may be an arrogant insistence on our own way, there may be the privilege and protection which a reputation for eccentricity may procure for a man, but there will be no Christian courage.

A missionary, recently returned to this country and having visited many ministers in many churches, remarked to a friend that never before in the history of Christianity had Christian ministers been gripped by so wide and so deep an uncertainty as they are now. This is one man's opinion, but the insight is uncomfortably accurate. Whatever it may say about our general ministry, it is a precise commentary on the state of our preaching. Is it not probable that our words are domesticated by the words of this world because we have too little confidence in the words which are not of this world? Is it not probably that Thomas' doubt stills more tongues for a longer time than Peter's denial?

Take that swift phrase which summarizes the whole gospel in five words: *Jesus Christ, Lord and Savior*. Do we believe it? How can we preach that Lord to our times with an earnestness which persuades other men unless we ourselves are confident that he will surely subject all things everywhere to his lordship? How can we preach that Savior unless we ourselves have the assurance which prepares us to surrender this world and this life in the faith that he has purchased for us another realm and another life? If we believe in a Lord from whose kingdom there is no honorable escape and from whose presence men can go out only into darkness, if we believe in a Savior who is powerful to save us from any disgrace with a forgiving love which endures beyond our last disobedience—if we are convinced of, and committed to, such a Lord and such a Savior, our preaching will not lack courage, pertinence, or urgency. As Bernard of Clairvaux so conclusively put it, "No words will avail to inspire hearers to celestial desire, which proceed from a cold heart. Nothing which does not burn itself can kindle flame in anything else."[2] This is well said but we do not have to surrender to a maxim, even when a Bernard of Clairvaux jams the gun in our ribs. Let us inquire further, and for ourselves, into the possibility that the decline of preaching is caused chiefly by our doubt about the urgency of the gospel. We are looking for something deeper than Bernard of Clairvaux's warm heart and kindled flame.

If our inquiry carefully scans good preaching from the pre-Christian beginnings of our faith to the present time, it will note that the sermons which had at their delivery the most effective impact and subsequently the most enduring influence were all drawn to the same basic pattern. Note carefully, however, that it is a pattern which has nothing to do with literary styles and sermonic types. Or, better said, the scheme present in every good sermon underlies and is antecedent to its literary form. Indeed, this essential, internal characteristic of the good sermon is sometimes so deeply imbedded and diffused that it becomes almost imperceptible. It lends itself to such a vast variety of uses that, like leaven in bread, it disappears in the grain and fabric of the good sermon, serving there invisibly. But it is always there; explicit or implicit, pronounced or muted, visible or hidden, this constant pattern is present in every good sermon. And always it is the absence or presence of this pattern rather than the absence or presence of a biblical text which determines whether a sermon is a sermon. It will be worth our while, therefore, to spend some time discovering and defining this design.

What is this indispensable something which, however deeply hidden, is always present in the good sermon and without which the sermon degenerates into a bloodless lecture or a trite moralism? Let us begin our search for it far off and with an apparently ridiculous illustration. Look at the distant kinsmen of the sermon, the second cousins once removed: dramas, novels, operas, and epic poems. In every one of them—from the *Iliad* to *The Death of a Salesman*, from the Greek chorus to *Madame Butterfly*—there is a constant factor, a basic assumption which gives all of them the family likeness. For each of these crafts cuts directly and vividly into the basic human conditions and sucks whatever vitality it has from the human drama. It portrays in one way or the other the elemental human situation and the perennial human struggle. It builds its playhouse on the real estate of human crises, on the crucial and invariant factors of human existence. These factors are: peril and promise and between the two, leading to the one or to the other, life's active agents. What is life? It is tragedy or, in the fine sense of the word, comedy, or an interweaving of the two, with the ultimate outcome hidden until the hero and the villain finish their battle and man goes with the victor to evil or to good.

Move still further from the sermon. Think of the blurred, gaudy, and maudlin reflections of dramatic art which we see in our favorite cowboy films, read in detective stories, and view in television's soap operas. We scoff at such melodramas not because they are basically false to life but rather because they burlesque the facts of life. But however comical the treatment and unrealistic the ending, the melodrama does assume the facts of the human struggle; it does draw upon the realities of the human situation, even though the happy ending is too easily contrived. For this, in burlesque, is always the human situation: the snarling villain at the door with the mortgage, the beloved family about to be dispossessed, and the timely or sometimes untimely arrival of the hero. This plot, however crudely it may be employed in some presentations, gropes its way nevertheless toward irreducible facts of the human drama: the peril, the promise, and the active agent.

Where else do we find this fundamental theme? We find it in the Bible. The Bible, in its first story about man, presents the alternatives which are to haunt him all his days: Eden or exile, life or death, and between the two God's command and forbidden fruit. And in the Bible's last story this same theme occurs as a man hears a voice, saying, "Let the evildoer still do evil, and the filthy still be filthy, and the righteous still do right, and the holy still be holy. Behold, I am coming soon, bringing my recompense, to repay every one for what he has done" (Rev. 22:11-12). And between these two stories the Bible is full of infinite variations of its central theme. It never tires of telling the story of the lost, the found, and the finder; the estranged, the reconciled, and the redeemer; the doomed, the saved, and the savior; the exiled, the restored, and the Messiah. The figure changes and we see Egypt, Canaan, and the exodus; Babylon, Jerusalem, and the return; a pigsty in a far country, a young man's memory, and a father's home; hell, heaven, and a cross. Indeed, does not the Bible itself, taken in the whole, rest upon this same plot in its eternal measurements? In a word, the Bible is the story of a lost child, facing an eternal lostness, offered an eternal home through Jesus Christ. Thus, starting afar off, we have now arrived at the Christian view of the fundamental theme of human existence: the Peril of God's wrath, the Promise of God's love, and the Option offered to all men in God's Son.

This theme, however it may vary in the intensity and explicitness of its declaration, is never missing in the good sermon. This is the primary and the ultimate test of whether or not a sermon is biblical, is Christian. Is man's plight or some phase of it declared? Is God's Promise or some part of it offered? Are Peril and Promise viewed in the light of God's revelation in Jesus Christ? In evangelistic and revival sermons this plot is boldly explicit. Take in outline, for example, one of Savonarola's sermons. He comes before the people of Florence, saying, "I preach the coming of the scourge. . . . The cup of your iniquity is full. . . . Repent and forsake evil. . . . Take the offered mercy. See! The cross is held out to you: come and be healed."[3] There it is: Peril, Promise and Alterant. But if you turn from such a starkly dramatic evangelist to this country's father of life-situation preaching, you do not find this theme left behind. You find it varied; you do not find it ignored. Henry Ward Beecher ends his sermon on "The Gentleness of God" with these words: "Will you be eternally beggared in the presence of an infinite supply? Will you wander eternally, homeless and lost, when your Father's house stands open, and all heaven cries to you 'Come!'?"[4] So, here too, the eternal plot in its biblical terms.

In the first paragraph of his first sermon in *Sermons Preached in a University Church*, Buttrick says, "Our human voyage is a still lonelier affair. The ship of this strange planet—should we say of the cosmos?—plunges on its way with no apparent port of departure, for nobody knows how or where or why our human life began; and no apparent port of arrival, for every passenger is buried in the deep. We are on a lonely voyage. When we confront that fact, biblical faith begins."[5] Thus his sermon emblazons against the black and forbidding mystery of the eternal sea an eternal light. Or, if we want a word closer to the young generation, this is what Dietrich Bonhoeffer said: "The whole purpose for which the Word came was to restore lost mankind to fellowship with God."[6] The evidence piles up; the more good sermons you read and the more that reading ranges over the whole history of Christian preaching, the more convinced you become that the sine qua non of the good sermon, of the biblical sermon, is the perennial and primordial theme of human existence: Man's Peril, God's Promise, and God's Act.

It is not suggested that we should appropriate and apply this theme from the outside, that by literary contrivances, affected voice, and the prefixing of an appropriate text we should work this pattern into our sermons to give a boost to our preaching. It is not suggested that the "preachableness" of a doctrine is the criterion of its truth. Such suggestions would make preaching an end rather than a means, an authority rather than a servant; it would make the act of proclaiming superior to the proclamation, the word *about* God paramount over God's Word. Dismiss at once any thought that you are being lured along a kind of utilitarian plane in search for something to preach that will restore virility to your preaching. But it is suggested that as Paul's descendants we cannot be merely "eager to preach"; we must be "eager to preach the gospel." Therefore, the primary question is not how to get the power of the human drama and its biblical interpretation into our preaching but rather how to restore in ourselves an urgent sense of the human Peril, confidence in the divine Promise, and trust in God's Power to transform the one into the other. When we once more believe what the gospel says about the horrors of the Peril and the beauty of the Promise and the adequacy of the Agent, all our eccentric theological and genteel literary precautions cannot prevent our preaching "as a dying man to dying men."

We can therefore make three definite and conclusive statements about good preaching. First, it always sounds the note of warning. Subtly or bluntly it raises a signal over the Peril or over some aspect of the Peril. It sounds the alarm; it cries "Danger, look out, beware"; it puts one on guard. If the sermon fails to do so, it is not faithful to the human situation; for the vulnerable life of man is immersed in a sea of troubles. If the sermon fails to sound the warning, it is not faithful to the listener: he is in great and grave danger; his flesh and his spirit are in jeopardy; he is confronted not merely by a minor inconvenience but by a major tragedy; and someone must tell him so or he perishes. And alas, if the sermon, as too often happens, lulls the listener into a false sense of security, if it whispers to the listener "All's well" when the world about him falls apart and the world within him explodes, then the sermon is not faithful to itself. It is worse than a deceiver; it is a traitor. And if the sermon fails its function as a warning, it is not faithful to the God who sets his ministers as watchmen in the night.

Note with what care we have used the word *warning* and with what deliberateness we have thus far avoided the word *threat*. These two words belong to the same family but they do not have the same meaning. To warn is to give notice of an approaching danger or evil; to threaten is to menace. The threat promises punishment for disobedience; the warning merely points out the punishment which is inherent in the disobedience. "Beware of the dog!" is a warning; "Trespass and we'll set our dogs on you!" is a threat. A sign posted in a field near Colorado Springs reads, "Watch out for rattlesnakes!" That is a warning. But when you hear the rattle of the snake, that is no polite warning—it is a threat.

The warning, however, is valid only when the peril is real. Post the Colorado Springs sign in the icy regions of the Arctic and it becomes comical. Men heed warnings only where there is at least an implied and believable threat. Somewhere in the child's experience incessant warning must be punctuated by punishment; cause must be followed by effect; or the warning becomes a farce. Better to give it up than to keep on promising the child a retribution he knows he will never receive. Is man's Peril real? Is there an evil which can be avoided? Can the minister expose the threat of that Peril in such a way that he himself does not become its agent? We must not lean so far away from the use of the threat that we fail to give the warning. As James Black pointed out in his *The Mystery of Preaching*, we have become "mealy-mouthed" in preaching about punishment. But as he put it, "The whole creation is grim with it. It is the one religious doctrine that has been buttressed by every discovery."[7] Our preaching must not be a moralistic "tut, tut"; it must show the pit gaping at the feet of sinful man.

The good sermon, to be sure, does not threaten; it does not hold hell over the heads of the listeners as a club and with that club beat the people into submission. The good sermon does not try to scare people into the church, away from their sins, or out of their money. But if there is not in the sermon a warning about hell or hell's equivalent, it is false to the people, to the realities of the human situation, to itself, and to the God who says to his messengers, "If I say to the wicked, 'You shall surely die,' and you give him no warning, nor speak to warn the wicked from his wicked way, in order to save his life, that wicked man shall die in his iniquity; but his blood I will require at your hand" (Ezek. 3:18).

It requires of us great care in our preaching to warn and yet not to encroach upon God's exclusive right to threaten, to identify the judgment without presuming to execute it, to speak of God's wrath without exhibiting man's revenge. But that is a part of the preacher's task and it can be done. Note the transformation which took place in the Apostle Paul. Before he traveled the Damascus road, even after he had watched Stephen stoned to death, Saul was "still breathing threats and murder against the disciples of the Lord" (Acts 9:1). It would be comforting if we could identify that mood exclusively with the ranting, fundamentalist evangelists. But in truth we cannot do so. Even in some genteel pulpits there is a subtle but brutal scourging of the people week after week, "breathing threats and murders against the disciples of the Lord." We find that kind of preaching repugnant and we should, but our wholesome desire to remove Saul from the Christian pulpit is no reason for keeping Paul out of it. Paul warned. He wrote to the Corinthians in his second letter, "I warned those who sinned before and all the others, and I warn them now while absent, as I did when present on my second visit, that if I come again I will not spare them—since you desire proof that Christ is speaking in me" (II Cor. 13:2–3b). And this is at least part proof that Christ is speaking in us, when we warn those whom Christ loves and to whom he has sent us.

Warn them of what? Well, for one thing we must warn our people of the dire consequences which alienation from God and disobedience to his will have upon *this* life. The Peril is current and it is present. The winds of God's wrath sweep through man's earthly affairs. So we must in faithfulness raise a signal over the wages of sin that are paid in this life. The eternal Peril breaks into the temporal realm in the form of wars, slums, racial strife, broken homes, political corruption, morbid and dying cultures. In the individual personal life, it appears in the form of anxiety, bitterness, emptiness, despair. Such are the dangers; they are real; they lurk in the shadows lining the narrowly lighted corridors of our private and our common life, waiting to pounce upon us.

Why should we who have something more to offer leave such warnings to the Camuses, the Bertrand Russells, and the angry young men who have nothing more to offer? Is it possible that the children of darkness see clearer than we do the nature of the abyss? They should not. Have we not read Paul? "For the wrath of God is revealed from heaven against all ungodliness and wickedness of men who by their wickedness suppress the truth" (Rom. 1:18). Do we flee from Paul to Jesus in the hope that in his teachings we shall find the Peril less horribly described? We are mistaken. "For behold, the days are coming when they will say, 'Blessed are the barren, and the wombs that never bore, and the breasts that never gave suck!' Then they will begin to say to the mountains, 'Fall on us'; and to the hills, 'Cover us' " (Luke 23:29–30). How can we who with Paul are apostles of this Christ ignore or mute his warning? So in faithfulness our preaching must alert men to the tragedies which haunt this life. We are the ones to do it, not the brilliant, courageous, and desperate humanists who have only bad news for mankind.

However, if the note of warning in our preaching is restricted to this world's affairs, if it merely points out the sociological and psychological dangers of man's estrangement from God, it will not be adequate. If there is in that warning no eschatological note which sees both the estrangement and its peril continuing beyond this life into the next, then the preaching will be superficial and the warning will lose much of its soberness. Indeed, in that case, it will be a deceptive preaching and a false warning. For this world, as the gospel sees it, is no sovereign, self-sufficient state completely isolated from the cosmos, with the God of the whole creation excluded by some kind of human interposition or divine withdrawal. This world is part of the main and what happens here has not merely cosmic but also supernatural and supertemporal reverberations. None of us knows all that the Apostle means by this strange phrase from the 8th Chapter of Romans: "For the creation waits with eager longing for the revealing of the sons of God. . . ." (Rom. 8:19a). But certainly he meant at least this, that the drama which is being played out here on earth is an essential part of a larger drama. Push this earth as far out to the edge of the universe as your cosmology requires, the earthly drama, Paul implies, is the key to all creation. So it is that in the quaint and tender words of Jesus we read that "there will be more joy in heaven over one sinner who repents than over ninety-nine righteous persons who need no repentance" (Luke 15:7b). Note how the words *in heaven* suggest a fatherland intimately, agonizingly involved in its colony's affairs. Nor is this temporal realm which we inhabit seen by the gospel as a snip of time cut off and separated from the eternal cloth. The tale that is told here did not begin here by spontaneous generation and it does not end here by the disappearance of man in death. There is an interpenetration of time and eternity. All of which is a way of saying that both the Peril and the Promise of the human drama extend beyond the final things of time and earth. The Peril is not merely temporal but is also ultimate.

To ignore this fact in our preaching and in particular to omit from our preaching the warning that God's wrath extends beyond time, is to preach a partial gospel. To be sure, it is a psychological and homiletical error to keep the Peril always in the forepart of the canvas, to paint the canvas big with the somber colors of despair. But it is a theological error to paint any picture of the human experience which does not have somewhere among its colors the warning shades of an outer darkness into which the soul of man may stray. A popular preacher, whose name you would have no difficulty guessing, said to his people, "Never think of death; push the thought of it out of your mind." The preacher erred, not knowing the scriptures. It is not God but the devil who says to man—says it to him even in his Eden—"You will not die" (Gen. 3:4b). If the minister would speak for God rather than for the devil, he will put into his preaching—stated or implied—the warning of God's threat against the insolently disobedient child.

We could camp here a long time pondering the scriptural and theological arguments for and against a doctrine of universal salvation. The arguments cut both ways. *Never* is a word we hesitate to ascribe to God's ability and his willingness to draw all of his children eventually to himself. Nor do we lightly apply the word *never* to a sovereign God's right and his will to exclude some of his children forever. The answer to this debate is securely wrapped in the mystery of the future, to which and to erudite journals of theology we should perhaps consign it. But if there is any continuity between this life and the next, if time in any way penetrates eternity, then there is no ground for the people's widespread and blasé assumption that the good and evil, the repentant and the unrepentant, will be indistinguishable and their recompense identical in the life that is to come. And our present concern is the effect of this everything-will-come-out-all-right-in-the-end mood on our preaching.

Herbert H. Farmer in his book *God and Men* took up this same question. But he put it down too quickly and too confidently. Arguing for a doctrine of universal salvation he wrote, "The second consideration which makes many hesitate to accept a doctrine of the final restoration of all persons is that they judge that such a doctrine takes away the urgency of the Christian message. . . ."[8] In part we must agree with Farmer's argument. Obviously we do not test the truth of a doctrine by the needs of a seminary's department of practical theology. Preaching, we have said, is no touchstone which proves the validity of doctrines. However, to conclude as Farmer did that a popular acceptance of a doctrine of general restoration does not diminish the urgency of the gospel and the zeal of preaching is to confuse what should happen with what does happen.

Let us take the least palatable illustration we can think of, the professional evangelist. If he believes unquestionably that one of his hearers, a lost soul, could leave the evening meeting, fall and break his neck on the church steps, die unrepentant, and spend eternity in a literal hell; if he believes without doubt that some word he speaks under God's appointment and by God's power could at the last moment snatch the unbeliever from his damning unbelief and turn him toward eternal bliss, there will be in his preaching a pleading and a passion which would otherwise be missing. But if you convince him that there will be in the great assize only a brief division of the sheep and the goats; that there is no outer darkness and will be no "weeping and wailing and gnashing of teeth"; that an indulgent, doddering God whose business it is to forgive mischievous children will eventually have every one of us for his own even though we stubbornly defy him; then there will seep out of his preaching much of the pressure which gave drive and impact to his words, urgency to his tone, and persuasiveness to his manner. Warning deflates into gentle admonition, judgment shrivels into carping moralism, pleading softens to genteel invitation, and a preacher dies. How can he sustain, as he would put it, a passion for lost souls now that he is convinced that they are not really eternally lost but only temporarily displaced?

To most of us this standard evangelistic approach is irksome, embarrassing, and repugnant. We need to ask why this is so. Is it because the evangelist's cosmology is unscientific or because his eschatology is expressed in the naïve terms of a flat, one-dimensional history? This is hardly the answer, unless we are ready to discard the writers of the New Testament along with the evangelist. Do we conclude that his stressing of the perils of hell and the glamor of heaven is merely a device to coerce the minds and hearts of men? (How can we be so certain that we always read the professional evangelist's motives correctly?) Do we write off the climactic plea of the evangelist's sermon as a fictitious horror story? (What rule forbids the use of fiction in the portrayal of fact?) No, what repels us in this typical evangelistic approach is none of these but rather the melodrama of this appeal. Not that it is false to the basic plot of human destiny but that it is a burlesque of that plot—that is what offends us. Intentionally or not, such spurious evangelism subjects the awesomeness of the human story and the grandeur of the divine purpose to ridicule and consequently to incredulity. The tragedy of such evangelism is not that it makes modern man believe in hell but that it makes hell unbelievable.

Now the question for us is whether we do as good a job as the evangelist in raising a signal over the punishment which dogs wicked and unregenerate man in this life and in the next. Do we have a theological equivalent for the evangelist's eternal damnation? Do we have a linguistic equivalent for the ceaseless fire in which the worm burns but is not consumed? Look at sophisticated, suburban man, propped up on all sides by status symbols. Is that man's soul in peril? Do you in your preaching warn him that the enemy pursues him or do you help him look the other way? That tough, worldly-wise dweller in the inner city and the housewife living out her innocent routine in a placid town and the young man just leaving home for college—how do you convince them that the seed of Peril is already planted in every cell of their being? How do you tell them of the tragedies and the ultimate tragedy which await them if they escape the God who seeks them? Do you warn them?

It is better to tell them, wiser and in the end kinder to warn them. The warning against the Peril and against the multiple out-croppings of that Peril in man's earthly affairs is certainly not the best news that we have for our people; but, again, it is not the worst. The worst news we can give our people is to preach as though God does not care what man does, is detached and dis-interested, looks on if at all in sovereign silence and unconcern. Forgiveness is best but punishment is better than neglect. This ex-plains why the guilty will sometimes morbidly seek punishment if its coming is delayed. The passion for meaning overpowers the urge to escape. Punishment is proof that God is holy, that he is right-eous, that there is meaning in his creation, that we are involved in that meaning even when we are on the wrong side of it. Much better is the preaching which acknowledges this fact than the preaching which leaves creation's throne empty. Better a Jonathan Edwards holding men like a spider over a flaming hell than a namby-pamby preacher who assures his people that they have no cause to fear God's wrath in this world or the next.

We conclude, then, that a note of warning sounds in every good sermon. It may be as boldly explicit and unmistakable as a patrol car's siren or as subtle and restrained as a father's word to his adult son. It may mark some minor crevice where the poisonous fumes break through the crusts of life into man's social, political, and domestic relationships. But it may—indeed sometimes must—warn of that wider, bottomless chasm into which the soul of man may plunge in eternal alienation from God or until God in his mercy cries "Enough!" But whatever the form or intensity of the signal, this is certain: no warning, no sermon.

Our attention thus far has been absorbed by one side of that eternal triangle—Peril, Promise, and the Divine Catalyst—which underlies the human drama. It is, we have seen, a triangle which

is assumed by all the arts and by the parodies of the arts, which in
the Bible is plunged and lifted to its supernatural and supertemporal measurements, and which—basic in human life and in God's
Word to life—is never absent from, or ignored by, the good sermon.
Our focus has been on that factor most neglected in modern
preaching—the Peril; the earthly and the cosmic, the present and
the ultimate threat of evil against the body, the community and the
soul of man. The threat is real; it is total; it endangers the inner
nature of man's being. It is the duty of the Christian preacher,
loving men as Christ loves them, to warn them as he warns them:
"I tell you, my friends, do not fear those who kill the body, and
after that have no more that they can do. But I warn you whom to
fear: fear him who, after he has killed, has power to cast into hell;
yes, I tell you, fear him!" (Luke 12:4-5).

We have seen, however, that the human drama does not move
on one leg. One part of that drama, man's Peril, is real; but it is
not the only reality. The Promise is also real and is also an essential
factor in the human struggle. If man's life had only one dimension
and that one tragic, if the happy outcome were impossible or un-
thinkable, there would be no drama, real or fictional. All drama,
even the magnificent Greek and Shakespearean tragedies, take for
granted the possibility of tragedy's counterpart. In it there is an
assumed peril and an implied promise. The drama which lacks
either factor collapses as a literary device not because the drama
requires suspense but because the drama in its basic plot must be
faithful to the human situation: life and death, good and evil,
blessing and curse. In theatrical terms life is a drama, not a farce;
whether it ends in good or evil, it makes sense.

Take, for example, one of the most melancholy works, a piece of
fiction which looks as deep into the abyss as any we know, Mel-

ville's *Moby Dick*. We find Melville's thesis in a line with as much
sheer despair in it as any in literature. "Though in many of its
aspects this visible world seems formed in love, the invisible spheres
were formed in fright." One of Melville's purposes in *Moby Dick*
was to prove this thesis. The whole book condenses into that scene
in which the whaling crew, after an unsuccessful and nearly dis-
astrous pursuit of the whale, is trying to return to the mother ship
in a small boat. The crew is cut off by storm and darkness and the
little boat is lashed and tossed by wind and wave. All attempts to
find the companion boats and the mother ship have failed. Then
it is that Starbuck finally lights the lantern and Queequeg holds
it aloft in the darkness on the waif pole. Note the storm and the
gloom and the darkness of the canvas as Melville paints it: "There,
then, he sat, holding up that imbecile candle in the heart of that
almighty forlornness. There, then, he sat, the sign and symbol of
a man without faith, hopelessly holding up hope in the midst of
despair."[9] That is Melville's picture of man: nothing overhead but
eternal darkness; nothing beneath but a cold, bottomless sea; nothing around to break the loneliness and share the terror; and rising
and falling with the heaving sea, a foolish candle of hope.

Yet *Moby Dick*, for all the terror throbbing in every pulse of it,
has a happy note at the end. In the epilogue Melville writes, "The
drama's done. Why then here does any one step forth?—Because
one did survive the wreck."[10] And looking back over the story we
remember that now and then across the path of Ahab's ship, the
Pequod, there had sailed another ship, the *Rachael,* mourning and
searching for her missing children. It was a reminder to the men
on the *Pequod* that somewhere there were sane men bent on a sensi-
ble mission. And after the wreck of the *Pequod* it was the *Rachael*
which found Ishmael, held up by a coffin life-buoy, floating life's
treacherous sea on a coffin.

We are not depending upon Herman Melville to tell us whether or not the "invisible spheres were formed in fright." We have another authority on that question. We are merely looking for the moment at the literary interpretation of the human struggle and are observing in fictional reflections on human destiny that tragedy is not really tragic unless it is offset by tragedy's opposite. And in no literature is this so evident as in the holy scriptures to which Melville's choice of names lead us. From the beginning of the Bible to the end there are alternate accounts of Peril and Promise: the exiled and the restored, the lost and the found, the kingdoms of men and the kingdom of God, the pit and a fair place high and lifted up. There are always two sides to the Bible's coin: blessing and curse, life and death, the saved and the perishing, heaven and hell, the cunning persistence of the devil and the unwearied love of God. And the purpose of the Bible is to convince us in language darker and brighter than man has used anywhere else of the reality and the ultimacy of both possibilities, to set the one against the other, to warn us of the Peril and assure us of the Promise, to threaten and to entreat us so that we may come from the outer darkness into the light and joy of the Father's house.

Nowhere in the Bible do we find the Promise flung against the Peril with such force and finality as we do in the writings of Paul. He dashed about over the rim of the Mediterranean with a cry on his lips and that cry was not "flee" but "come." Against the immensity and the depth of man's sin he threw his confidence in the power of God's redeeming grace in Jesus Christ. He challenged the Peril—a threat to man in this life and the next—with the proclamation that the rescuing power of God is more than a match for the terrors of man's predicament. To men who asked of him, "What must I do to be saved?" he replied, "Believe in the Lord Jesus, and you will be saved, you and your household" (Acts

16:31). Where men were not jarred by an earthquake into the realization that they were lost, he showed them in men's affairs and in men's souls the seismographic tracings which warned of the coming earthquake and, having warned them, lured them toward safety in the free gift of God. He was no Cassandra whose warnings, incessantly repeated, made men despair and eventually disbelieve; he was a messenger sent by the highest authority on an errand of good news to desperate men. If he said, "By your hard and impenitent heart you are storing up wrath for yourself on the day of wrath when God's righteous judgment will be revealed" (Rom. 2:5), he also said, "There is therefore now no condemnation for those who are in Christ Jesus" (Rom. 8:1).

We are ready to make our second definite and conclusive statement about good preaching. The good sermon always presents the Promise over against the Peril. If this definition suggests the necessity for a rigid, standardized sermonic outline, a required style, it is misunderstood. The essentials of the sermon, as we saw earlier, have to do with literary styles and homiletical types only in the sense that these essentials find their expression in a variety of sermonic patterns and in a multiplicity of literary devices. To suggest that the good sermon confronts the Peril with the Promise is not to require the drafting of a particular form of sermon. We are not thinking of the skeleton of the sermon or of the flesh hanging on its bones. We are thinking of its invigorating essence. At this level it does not matter whether the sermon is textual, expository, topical, evangelistic, or what not. Here it does not matter whether the sermon falls into three parts, two or one. What does matter is this: Does the sermon warn men of the danger in which sin and mortality submerge his whole being? Does the sermon hold out to such a man the promise of God's redeeming and resurrecting love?

To say that God addresses his Promise to our total earthly condition—to all the glory and the wretchedness of our personal and our common life—is simply to declare the truth of the gospel. The Promise is God's universal and sufficient gift of his will, his love, and his power through his Son to needful man in all his conditions. Jesus' word "I came that they may have life, and have it abundantly" (John 10:10b) may refer in part to the ultimate and to the other-worldly; but it also has fulfillments in this life within the bounds of the here and now. How absurd it is, then, for a congregation to ask a minister to preach the gospel and yet forbid him to throw the warning and the plea of the gospel against man's whole psychic and social experience. God counters the Peril with his Promise wherever the Peril appears. This being so the preacher cannot preach the gospel in this day with passion and in its wholeness without reference to race prejudice and oppression, alcoholism, divorce, the secular idolatries, the modern and domestic breeds of tyranny, and man's suicidal race toward nuclear war. The threat to man's soul and his society is ultimate but it is also immediate. Whatever face the evil one may wear in the life to come, in this life the Peril appears in the brokenness of the inner man and in all shatterings of the human oneness. It confronts man wherever and whenever in his personal or communal life he offends God. Therefore, we can talk about a personal gospel and a social gospel only for academic purposes. The gospel is indivisible. It is God's simultaneous warning and entreaty to the whole man.

Therefore, we preach a gospel which is not of this world but which must be preached to this world. In that preaching we chase a frantic man who is madly fleeing in all directions but the right one to escape emptiness, anxiety, and despair about himself and his brother. By every available means of communication we overtake him and offer him God's Promise: cleansing and purging for his guilt; meaning in place of his bewilderment; purpose for his scattered, random, and conflicting purposes; healing for his wounds and reconciliation to his God and his brother. Man wanders like a lost child in a forest full of wild beasts, and God's minister is a ranger sent to find him and to speak the Word and show the way which lead home. We are entrusted with that Word and that way which in this world lead to life. Frail and inadequate as we know ourselves to be, we are commissioned nevertheless to proclaim the Promise.

This is a serious business and a grave responsibility—far more so than the doctor's treatment of the physical body or the statesman's ministry to the political body. Unless the Promise is acceptably preached, long life, good health, and strong government can add to, rather than diminish, the Peril. Let the world with its distorted evaluations push the preaching profession as far down the status scale as it wishes; let other men pursue rank if they will. The fact remains that God has entrusted to the chosen preacher of his Word the proclaiming of his utmost gift to his most needful child. Whether this chosen preacher serves a rural parish in North Dakota or First Church in some teeming city, God's Word through him can mean the difference between life and death, blessing and curse. If he believes this, as he should, then his service through the preached word becomes the most exciting, demanding, zealous, and rewarding career entrusted to any man. If he himself has faced the immensity of the Peril and accepted the ampleness of the Promise, he knows, whatever the world may say, that he has been seized by God for a mission with which none other can be compared.

Still he is humble. He knows that the Promise is not his to offer or to execute. He knows that he is an earthen vessel, that he is expendable. And he knows that the efficacy of the Promise in this life is neither as demonstrable or as mechanical or as predictable as the heart of sophisticated, practical man desires. God's concern, his love, and the moving of his Spirit in our lives cannot be proved by discovering a biblical text for each exigency of life. The Bible in the lonely hotel room, with its appended menu of scriptural passages for moods and occasions, offers poor fare at best if the reader of it does not grasp the totality of God's act toward him. God's Promise is not à la carte—dish by dish with a stated price for each item; it is a lavish, free banquet for all who will come, eat, and drink.

Nor do we demand of the Promise that it prove in advance how it is equal to each vicissitude of this life; rather, we accept in trust that it is equal to all of them. The Promise, when received, does not take away the pain, the mystery, the agony, and the struggle of human existence. But it does lift all of them—even life's most distressing ironies and perplexities—into the meaningfulness of God's purpose. We know that everything does not turn out all right in this world, but also "we know that in everything God works for good with those who love him, who are called according to his purpose" (Rom. 8:28). And this is what we preach when we preach the Promise to this age. We ministers are not medicine men with black bags full of specific nostrums, one for each and every ill which befalls man in this world. It is foolish to pretend that we are, dangerous to preach as though heaven were a cosmic pharmacy and we were writers of prescriptions. What we do have is a gospel which declares the will of God for men in this life and which sets before them in all the affairs of this life the curse and the blessing.

The Peril against which we warn men is both immediate and ultimate; the Promise which as God's messengers we declare to men is both present and eternal. Try as we may—if we are so disposed—we cannot eliminate from the imagination of man nor from the scriptures the repetitious thought and phrase, "and in the life to come." What about the life to come? Sophistication may hide the question but it neither cancels nor answers it. The question remains; indeed, it is the key question. And the way it is answered throws light or darkness upon our earthly life. If the Promise is only temporarily a match for the Peril, if it cannot speak a final No to death, to eternal nothingness, to perpetual estrangement from God, then it offers us a hollow victory, an armistice after which the Peril is in complete command. The devil, then, is released not merely for a thousand years but forever. In this mood Paul wrote to the Corinthians, "If Christ has not been raised, your faith is futile and you are still in your sins" (I Cor. 15:17). Indeed so! We must preach the resurrected Christ and the promise of an eternal life in him, not as an afterthought, not as the decorative copestone of our faith, but as the forethought of God, the foundation of our faith on which the whole rests. Easter Sunday should be for us merely the day on which there gushes forth with all its power and healing a mighty stream which during all the year flows beneath and through the church's calendar.

Warning and good news are not the whole of the gospel; there is a third indispensable part to which we now come. But these are two of the essential parts of the gospel's trilogy and consequently and essentially they are two parts of the good sermon. So we must ask of each sermon we preach whether or not in some way faithful to the gospel it sets God's Yes over against his No. Does it in some unmistakable way let Christ say "I tell you, fear him" and does it against that saying raise Christ's "Fear not, little flock, for it is your Father's good pleasure to give you the kingdom" (Luke 12:32)? Have you noticed in the gospel of Mark and of Luke the juxtaposition of the story of the rich young man and the story of the little children who were taken into Christ's loving arms? Shakespeare noticed this parallel and made much of it in King Richard II:

> *The better sort,—*
> *As thoughts of things divine,—are intermix'd*
> *With scruples, and do set the word itself*
> *Against the word:*
> *As thus,—"Come, little ones"; and then again,—*
> *"It is as hard to come as for a camel*
> *To thread the postern of a small needle's eye."*

The whole gospel—all three parts of it: theme, countertheme, and middle term—are lodged in these two stories and in their proximity to each other. This is the gospel: on the one side a man turning from the Christ and the stern word following him, "Children, how hard it is to enter the kingdom of God!" (Mark 10:24b), and on the other side the children flocking to Christ at his gentle word, "Let the children come to me, do not hinder them; for to such belongs the kingdom of God" (Mark 10:14b). How hard, how easy! What sorrow, what joy! How perilous it is to be radically confronted by Jesus Christ, yet how great the Promise in such confrontation.

Thus we approach the third definite and conclusive statement which we can make about the interior design of the good sermon. We have seen that in drama and melodrama there is always an implied or explicit tension created by the opposed alternatives, Peril and Promise. We have noted that this is not an artificial literary invention but is an accurate reflection of the Peril-Promise motif which runs through the whole human struggle. We have discovered that this motif, expressed in its most radical terms, is the constant theme of the biblical drama and therefore must be repeated in one way or the other in the biblical sermon. Now we must add a third strand to this central cord running through drama, Bible, and the human struggle.

In the literary field drama and melodrama always employ a key which swings the plot one way or the other, a dramatic interchange which sends the action of the play toward ruin or toward a happy solution of the particular human predicament. A case of mistaken identity, the accidental drinking of a deadly potion, the caprice of the Fates, the timely arrival of Hairbreadth Harry—on such literary hinges the drama turns. And this, too, is no artificial device. Rather it accurately reports the decisive role which things, people, and events play in the unfolding issues of the human adventure. In the biblical drama the active agent, the determinative Alterant, is God. Sometimes the Hebrew people thought that he had withdrawn completely to the far-off top of his mountain; at other times they saw his powerful hand in the thick of their affairs. But their response to him, whether they saw him or not, determined again and again in biblical history whether God's people suffered the Peril or inherited the Promise.

When the biblical drama moves from the Old Testament to the New, the key to the human story is specifically identified. The New Testament declares that the key, the active agent, the Alterant poised between ruin and blessing, is one man, God's Son, Jesus Christ. So repetitious, so sharply focused, so exclusive is this testimony that almost any New Testament verse will serve as its proof. Take one, Paul's word in his Second Letter to the Corinthians: "For the Son of God, Jesus Christ, whom we preached among you, Silvanus and Timothy and I, was not Yes and No; but in him it is always Yes. For all the promises of God find their Yes in him" (II Cor. 1:19-20b). Or to pick another Pauline verse, take the words the Apostle wrote to the Romans immediately following his dark description of the guilt and lost condition of man: "But now the righteousness of God has been manifested apart from law, although the law and the prophets bear witness to it, the righteousness of God through faith in Jesus Christ for all who believe" (Rom. 3:21–22b). There is Peril; Paul does not blink it; but, for all who believe, Jesus Christ is God's "But now!"

If, then, the good sermon warns men of the threatening Peril and declares to them the assured Promise, it must also proclaim the Alterant operating decisively between the two. The good sermon dare not leave the people either comfortably or miserably suspended between an unconfronted Peril and an ungrasped Promise. It cannot leave them wondering how the horrors of so great a Peril can be escaped and how the blessings of so good a Promise can be obtained. However good such a technique may be in other settings, the sermon is not an exercise in nondirective counseling. On the contrary, the sermon proclaims, declares, specifies; it is boldly indicative and declarative. However much we may warn men of the Peril and offer them the Promise, we have not preached the gospel until we proclaim to men that One who transforms Peril into Promise for those who believe in him, until we have declared to them that Christ in whom "all the promises of God find their Yes. . . ."

Indeed, what else do we have to offer men who dawdle between the pigsty on one side and their Father's home on the other? We are not sociologists, psychologists, or political scientists; we are proclaimers of the redeeming and reconciling act of God in Jesus Christ for the whole fabric of the human experience. However many ways we may need to turn the sermon so that it penetrates the curtains men draw against it, however wide the application, this is the good news we proclaim to men: that "God was in Christ reconciling the world unto himself" and that "there is therefore now no condemnation for those who are in Christ Jesus."

Something, we must admit, has stolen from us the eagerness and the gladness of that proclamation. Assuming that we believe that the Peril and the Promise are both real and live alternatives, why is there so little joy and zeal in the preaching of that Alterant in whom the one condition is transformed into the other? Consider two possibilities. Is it not something more than a coincidence that the decline of urgent preaching has been paralleled by the rise of the church school? To answer Yes to this question is neither to condemn the church school nor to repudiate the pulpit. For it is not the church school as such which threatens preaching. Religious education has become and should remain an indispensable function of the church. At its best it is not the pulpit's enemy or its competitor or its substitute. Rather, the preaching of the gospel is hampered by the popularizing of a particular philosophy of religious education. There is a popular theory of Christian education which assumes an automatic continuity between parent and child, home and child, church school and child. It assumes that the faith which dwells in the grandmother, Lois, and in the daughter, Eunice, will by inheritance dwell in the grandson, Timothy. This theory assumes, therefore, that the need for repentance and conversion can be eliminated by religious training. The people's acceptance of such a theory and the minister's acquiescence in that acceptance will dull the edge of his preaching of Jesus Christ as Lord and Savior. This is a way of saying that Horace Bushnell's *Christian Nurture*, valuable as its insights may be in some areas, nevertheless has had a deleterious effect upon the American pulpit. The gist of Bushnell's theory can be put in a few of his own words: "What is the true idea of Christian education? . . . That the child is to grow up a Christian and never know himself as being otherwise."[11] If this theory is accepted, then—except for its appeal to those people who have not had the benefits of such Christian nurture—the pulpit becomes merely an adjunct of the church school.

It can be said just as categorically, however, that until a man knows that he is *not* a Christian, until he acknowledges an utter discontinuity between himself and God, he cannot become a Christian. It is a function of the sermon to stir in men a sharp awareness of this discontinuity; to show any man, however boastfully and truthfully he can say "All these I have observed from my youth," that he stands even yet before One who can say to him, "You lack one thing. . . ." If on the other hand we ministers concede that it is enough to push the child in at one end of the church school and eject him at the other with church membership stamped on him mechanically somewhere in between, with nothing happening to the child along the way but the accumulation of religious knowledge punctuated occasionally by minor emotional crises, then we underestimate the complexity and the depth of the human soul and the uniqueness of the claim God makes upon it. If we believe that such religious training at its best is not only a substitute for, but also an improvement on, the preached gospel, then our preaching will become pedagogic and the prophetic cut and fire will go out of it. We must do everything we can through the home and the church school to bring up the children "in the discipline and instruction of the Lord," but we must remember that there is something more important than discipline and instruction, something which discipline and instruction, if mismanaged, can obstruct: the soul's own direct confrontation by the God who breaks through all shells—including the insulation of formal religious training—with his shattering No and his healing Yes.

Obviously the church school can and should be as thorough in its teaching and as correct in its doctrine as the pulpit is in its preaching. The pulpit does not have exclusive possession of the gospel or of Christian doctrine. The Peril-Promise-Alterant motif which the pulpit must preach, must also be the foundation of religious education. Here, of course, this theme is less explicit and less sharply focused than it is in the sermon. But if the church school cultivates moods and convictions which obscure the crisis in the human struggle, or if it offers men an easy journey through religious training into full communion with God, then the prophecy of the pulpit and the pedagogy of the church school are pulling in opposite directions. In such a tug of war it is the pulpit which usually succumbs. Why preach the terror of the crisis and the commingled shame and glory of the cross and the agony and joy of a transformed life to men and women who can be gently nudged through Christian nurture into God's favor?

There is a second and more critical explanation of the evaporation of eagerness and urgency from our preaching of Jesus Christ as the divine and decisive Alterant between the Peril and the Promise. Let us approach that explanation by way of the New Delhi Assembly of the World Council of Churches. Far in advance of this meeting of the churches "Jesus Christ, the Light of the World" was selected as the general theme for the Third Assembly. This text, drawn from John 8:12 and related passages, was studied in the parishes of the member churches of the World Council for nearly a year before the Assembly. They were therefore the beacon which drew nearly sixteen hundred participants to New Delhi in the closing days of November and the early days of December, 1961. From all over the world across theological, traditional, creedal, geographic, ethnic, organizational, racial, and political lines Christians gathered to discuss, to serve, and to honor Jesus Christ as the Light of the World. Yet from the very first day of the assembly this theme diminished and others took its central place. Why so?

There are many answers to this question, but one of them points to the overriding concern of the Assembly to protect at all costs the Council's new-gained unity, scope, and strength. The prevailing spirit of the New Delhi Assembly was one of cautious deference, extreme courtesy, studied harmony, and the evading of such controversial subjects as the uniqueness of Jesus Christ. The mood of amiability was intensified by the Assembly's setting. India itself—a land of gracious and tolerant people—posed a problem for the Assembly. It was not the words *Jesus Christ* which troubled the delegates in the Indian setting. The delegates would not have been there if they had not in one way or the other already confessed their faith in Jesus Christ as God and Savior. Nor was it the word *Light* which made the Assembly vacillate and temporize, for this is an appellation traditionally applied to Jesus Christ. Nor was it the word *world*. Christianity is a "worldly" religion. No, the problem center, the monkey wrench in the Assembly's machinery, was the tiny, tough article *the*. Should the Assembly stress it or let it glide, write it big or set it small? Should they say lightly and vaguely "Jesus Christ, *Light* of the World"—an easy out in a land of many lights? Or should they say "Jesus Christ, *the* Light of the World" and face the charges of bigotry and exclusiveness?

The World Council of Churches is not here under censure. Its Central Committee is already taking bold steps to correct the errors of New Delhi by affirming and proclaiming "the finality of Jesus Christ in an age of universal history." The ambiguity which the Third Assembly permitted to settle like a fog around its central theme cannot be wholly blamed on the officers of the World Council. On the contrary, this is a mood which tempts the whole church and which rises from something much more serious than an amiable and genteel manner or a courteous tolerance. Our unwillingness to strike the note of uniqueness in proclaiming the Christian gospel flows not only from a deferent concern for the feelings of other people but even more from our own doubts about the finality of Jesus Christ. Kenneth Hamilton in his book *The Protestant Way* said that "the basis for toleration lies in doubt. What is certain does not allow of difference in interpretation. . . ."[12] Hamilton is wrong in suggesting that toleration can exist only where there is doubt about one's own position. But he is right in suggesting that doubt often underlies toleration. This may be our case. We do not insist upon the uniqueness and the sufficiency of Jesus Christ, we do not preach him as utterly different and final, because, consciously or not, we have our doubts about Jesus Christ. This is evident in the extent to which the modern pulpit lets syncretism lure it, in the degree to which it lets cult blend with culture, in the diminishing areas to which it is willing to apply the ethics of a Christ who is Lord as well as Savior.

This age, distinct as it is from all other ages, demands no new gospel but an old one, no eclectic religion but the singular, pristine gospel of Jesus Christ. Through all time and all space one thing is constant: creation's need and the Creator's response; the runaway child and the seeking Father; the evil that scatters and the Love that gathers all things to itself; man and God and the Christ who is "the same yesterday, today, and forever." The gospel we were appointed to preach is a blunt, unapologetic claim that Jesus Christ is *the* Light of the world—timeless, universal, final, sufficient. Jesus Christ is not merely a star of greatest magnitude in a constellation of similar though lesser stars; he is the light itself which the brightest stars only dimly reflect.

Such an accent upon the uniqueness of Jesus Christ and upon the exclusiveness of his claim is understandably offensive to the followers of other religions and understandably difficult to preach. To the non-Christian it is sheer arrogance. If from our side Jesus Christ is in truth the "only begotten Son of the Father," from their side this conviction is lumped with similar claims of other zealots. If we believe Jesus Christ when he says "*I* am the light of the world," they in turn call such an audacious claim the ranting of a megalomaniac. If we say with the Apostle "at the name of Jesus every knee should bow . . . and every tongue confess that Jesus Christ is Lord, to the glory of God the Father" (Phil. 2:10–11), they reply, "Thank you for your offer and for your frankness. We bow to other names and confess other lords."

Our purpose in the proclamation of the uniqueness and the sufficiency of Jesus Christ is not to preen ourselves or to offend the devotees of other faiths; our purpose is to declare the truth as it has been revealed to us and as we have been commanded to do. And this purpose becomes for Christ's appointed ministers a sacred duty and a glad one. We are neither proud of ourselves nor ashamed of the gospel. As arrogant as he may at times have seemed, the Apostle was nevertheless extraordinarily humble. His boast was in Christ, not in himself: "But we have this treasure in earthen vessels, to show that the transcendent power belongs to God and not to us" (II Cor. 4:7). The brilliant Hindu intellectual and vice-president of India, Radhakrishnan, has said, "Christians are an ordinary people who make extraordinary claims." Exactly! Whether he meant this definition to be derisive or not it describes perfectly what we Christians should be and specifically what we ministers are. We are ordinary people. To approach the non-Christian world believing anything else, posing as anything else, is to validate the charge that we are bigots. Our faith makes us superior to no people and our failure to keep the terms of that faith makes us inferior to no people. We do not offer the non-Christian *our* religion; we offer him what we believe should be *his* religion.

We ministers are earthen vessels, ordinary people, and each extension of our ordinary ministerial humanness is an expendable vessel: our ecclesiastical architecture, our church polity, our hymnology, our religious art, our political philosophy, and the intellectual systems which are for us the plinths upon which the faith rests—

these are all earthen vessels. We can glorify God in gothic, colonial, and free form churches but they are not essential to the glorification of God. We can praise Jesus Christ in "A Mighty Fortress" and "Love Divine, All Love Excelling" but these hymns can be replaced. We require harmony in prelude, anthem, and postlude; but there is music which, though innocent of harmony, need not be lacking in worship. We find democracy more favorable to Christianity than any other political system, but Christianity has lived under all political systems. We formalize the truth we have received in philosophical systems which have an Hellenic origin, but there are other philosophical systems which can catch the same revealed truth.

Nevertheless, we make—or we should—extraordinary claims, audacious claims. We claim as the scriptures do that Jesus Christ is the incomparable, irreplaceable, indispensable Alterant between the world's Peril and God's Promise. He is brother to every man and yet different from any man; son of Adam as we are sons of Adam, yet Son of God as no one of us is Son of God. It has to be admitted that so far as rivals, aids, and duplicates are concerned, the Christian faith is imperial, arbitrary, and intolerant. So it is not an easy thing for us to do: to be refined, sensitive to the feelings of other people, aware of our own disgraceful failures, alert to the good God stores in every life and still to preach the exclusive and astounding claims of the Christian gospel. But this is what we Christian ministers have been set apart to do.

There is a radical difference between lights and darkness, however dim the lights, however deep the darkness. Christian ministers therefore welcome and co-operate with all lights wherever they shine—in the face of the Jew who sells us a suit of clothes and while he does so earnestly talks of God's justice, in the atheist whose lack of faith we pity but whose dedication to humanity puts us to shame, in the Jehovah's Witness who lets his religion—whatever we may think of it—permeate his whole being. A light is a light and it is blasphemy to call it darkness. But there is also a radical difference between lights and *the* Light, between God's sons and his Son, between holy men and Jesus Christ. Jesus Christ is the Light and it is blasphemy for Christian ministers in their preaching to confuse him with the lights. Luke 12:8–9 may be as some say only "a christological designation read into the tradition by the early church."[13] Or it may be one of the primitive sayings of Jesus. Whichever it is, where else in Christian literature do Peril and Promise come into sharper focus and into more direct conflict than in these words addressed specifically to the disciples of Christ: "And I tell you, every one who acknowledges me before men, the Son of man also will acknowledge before the angels of God; but he who denies me before men will be denied before the angels of God" (Luke 12:8–9)? The pulpit cannot escape the plot which catches up all human history. It, too, is poised as the pew is between Peril and Promise, the outcome turning, as it does everywhere else, on its response to the Alterant, its reply to God's act in Jesus Christ.

3

The Meaning of Relevant Preaching

Theme, countertheme, and middle term; Peril, Promise, and Alterant; the wrath of God, the love of God, the gift of God—this is the design which underlies and the motif which permeates every good sermon. Against this background we can place the current debate on the need for relevancy in our preaching. There are two sides to this question and thoughtless, sometimes absurd statements have been made on both sides. There are preachers and teachers who insist—and rightly—that a living gospel should always be preached to a live situation. This side argues that one cannot preach the gospel to twentieth-century New York in the same way that it was preached to sixteenth-century London and that the difference involves something vastly more than the translation of an Elizabethan language into American vernacular. But to this there are preachers and teachers who reply—and rightly— that the gospel is inherently applicable to man in any of his situations and that attempts to adapt it only block or impair it. Is it not possible that each of these assumptions is correct but that each has been pushed to an extreme and false conclusion?

In his translation of the Pentateuch, Martin Luther wrote, "I endeavored to make Moses so German that no one would suspect he was a Jew." Undoubtedly this takes the zeal for relevancy too far.

But Luther's excessiveness at this point is refreshing in a day when an increasing number of homileticians chide the concern and the effort of preachers to make their sermons pertinent to the day in which those sermons are preached. The theory is that the proclaimed Word needs only to be proclaimed since it carries in itself the power to relate itself to the needs of all men in all times. It follows, according to this theory, that an exploration of man's heart and an analysis of the current situation are unnecessary and efforts to shape the proclaimed gospel to the analyzed situation are absurd. So runs the thought of those who rebuke all talk of relevancy and communication.

Exhibit A in this school is Dietrich Ritschl's *A Theology of Proclamation*. One of the fallacies of this exciting book is the author's unfortunate assumption that his knowledge of the church in Europe qualifies him to speak authoritatively to the church in the United States; the result is a breakdown in communications. But this is beside the point. In this book Ritschl says, "The content is what matters; and technique will grow out of the content, not vice versa."[1] Change *will* to *should* in that statement, say the same thing with the precaution H. Grady Davis uses in his *Design for Preaching*, and the assumption is correct. As it stands in Ritschl's words it is not correct. Content will not produce the right form and technique any more than an untended apple tree will naturally produce succulent and wormless apples.

Ritschl's approach to preaching raises serious questions about the apppropriateness of any attempt to apply what we preach to the contours of our age. This is an extreme view which runs counter to what most of us have been taught about the purpose of the sermon, and the intemperateness of this opinion can be in part explained—though not dismissed—on the basis of the theological presuppositions out of which it rises. But it is also a wholesome

recoil against the kind of life-situation preaching in which, to paraphrase P. T. Forsyth, we not only preach to our age but also preach
our age. Not all topical and life-situation sermons have fallen into
this trap to be sure; but so many have that the rebuke is needed
and should be graciously accepted. Too much of our preaching is
merely a pleasant conversation which our culture carries on with
itself.

Let us admit that we cannot *make* the gospel relevant. Few of
us, despite the fact that an occasional slip of the tongue sometimes
brings such words to our lips, believe that we can do so. We know
that the gospel is either germane or not and we know that the way
we handle it cannot make it one thing or the other. But to admit
that the gospel is God's Word to all men in all ages and that it is
valid whatever we do to it is not to solve the problem of the relevancy of the ministry, of preaching, or of the church. The actuality
and the vitality of the gospel do not prevent the ministry from
being superficial, the sermon from being impertinent, or the church
from being peripheral. It is folly in our preaching to assume that
substance automatically and inevitably finds its most efficient structure. It is irresponsible to assume that content inerrantly evolves
into proper form and technique. It is a dereliction on our part to
assume that the message for which we have been made the wit-
nesses will in spite of us become flesh and dwell among men. Life,
too, is an actual and vital force; it has an inner creative reality;
nevertheless, there are aberrant, useless, and ineffective forms of life.
If in our preaching we depend solely upon the actuality and vitality
of the gospel and are indifferent to the problems of communication,
we can expect that the gospel will be maimed and muted by the
aberrant and useless forms which we permit it to take. The preacher
is never an artist; that is, he never brings any new thing into being
through his preaching. But he is an artisan, a craftsman, whom

God has selected to declare a new thing to his people. He should therefore be as good a workman as he can.

In many studies today the heavy stress falls on the necessity for a preaching which is biblical and which considers itself a form of the Word of God and part of the redemptive act of God in Jesus Christ. This is not merely a healthful corrective of the errors into which topical, life-situation, moralistic preaching drifted, not merely a return of the pendulum, but is a deliberate claim that Christian preaching is a unique form of public proclamation, distinguished primarily by the conversation which it establishes between the hearer and the God of the Bible. So long as this emphasis does not itself degenerate into a fad and become an end in itself, submerging biblical preaching in a sea of jargon about biblical preaching, it is wholesome. The accent on biblical preaching, on preaching which is itself a Word of God, is good and proper. But whence comes the concomitant notion that such preaching must contemptuously spurn all elegance in written and spoken style? Who says that the biblical sermon must wear sackcloth and ashes, walk barefooted and eat only locusts and wild honey? Who set up the false dichotomy between the aesthetic and the useful, the beautful and the purposeful, the artful and the true?

Even the words *taste, style, elegance*—however masculine we make their definition—have fallen into disrepute as though taste had to do solely with the dandy's relish, style solely with the fashionable, and elegance solely with the artificial. But this notion— when it is carried over to the sermon and made the sermon's justification for dullness, awkwardness, and literary cheapness—will not do. It has no New Testament precedent; it certainly has no champion in the memorable sermons produced by the church over the centuries. It is indeed a blatant denial of the preacher's obligations to be diligent in his business and to study to show himself approved unto God. Moreover, if the preacher takes into his study and into his pulpit the idea that shoddy work will do so long as he speaks the truth in love, then he desecrates the only instruments he has: his language and his voice.

In a recent Tiffany & Co. advertisement, the company's chairman, Walter Hoving, wrote, "The unfortunate truth is that fewer and fewer young people seem to have an understanding of taste, and that is true of a great many older people as well." Mr. Hoving uses the word *taste* in one of its strict dictionary definitions: "the power of discerning and appreciating fitness, beauty, order, or whatever constitutes excellence, especially in the fine arts and belles-lettres; critical judgment, discernment, or appreciation." Taking the word in this strict sense we can say that the criticism, a rare technique among advertisers, cuts across our whole cultural scene. Not merely in jewelry—most of us cannot afford Tiffany anyway—but also in music, drama, dancing, architecture, art, and literature the public demand betrays the loss of taste. And the question for the preacher is whether in his sermon preparation and in his preaching he shall pander to this loss of the aesthetic sense and, indeed, by careless workmanship contribute to the loss.

It has been granted, and we should never lose sight of the fact, that in the sermon moral principles are to be preferred to pure aestheticism and that doctrines take priority over the espousal of moral principles. On a descending scale of homiletical requisites elegance, literary excellence, appears far down the ladder. Even John A. Broadus, who in his *On the Preparation and Delivery of Sermons* paid some attention to these things, did not deal with the style of the sermon—which he made Part IV of his work—until he had dealt with such matters as the text, doctrine, and the preacher's personal needs. And in this fourth part he made sermonic elegance tertiary to clarity and energy. So the argument is not that literary excellence should be sought as an end in itself. The argument, rather, is that no preacher who is anxious to convey God's message to the people with precision, energy, and persuasion can afford to spurn or to treat indifferently the instruments which God has made available. Chief among those instruments is that rich, precise, varied, and beautiful language that we are heir to.

It is an instructive fact that the most offensive sentences in the Bible—offensive in their collision with the people of ancient and present times—translate into beautiful and powerful English: "The lion has roared, who will not fear? The Lord God has spoken, who can but prophesy?" (Amos 3:8). "You brood of vipers! Who warned you to flee from the wrath to come?" (Luke 3:7b). "Claiming to be wise, they became fools, and exchanged the glory of the immortal God for images resembling mortal man or birds or animals or reptiles" (Rom. 1:22–23). Paul spurned the "enticing words of man's wisdom." Nevertheless, he put the power of excellent language at the disposal of the gospel. And, to the best of our ability, so should we.

In this connection it is odd that modern, sophisticated homileticians in citing the paragons of preaching always point to Peter and to Paul and never refer to Jesus of Nazareth. One reason for this omission is plain. In his preaching Jesus violated every rule which the latest schools of homiletics lay down in their doctrinaire definition of a sermon. More frequently than not in his preaching, the Prophet of Galilee used no text, appealed to nature for his illustrations, used direct counseling, preached topical sermons—in each instance doing what the modern vogue strictly and sanctimoniously forbids. But "the common people heard him gladly" for "never man spake like this man." With text or without text; heaping moral on moral; drawing his message and his opportunity from the setting as he looked round about him; picking illustrations from the ground—the fig tree, the lily, the fox; never without a parable; always by word of mouth—that is the way he preached. There are some twentieth-century theologians who think the less of him for it.

The record of the preaching and teaching of Jesus is often preceded by such words as "seeing the multitudes. . . . And he looked round about on them which sat about him." This is to say that Jesus took note of the people; he met them where they were; he took account of their need. Though there was an abundance of solid food, he sometimes, like Paul, gave them milk. Though the eons would collide in his life, he talked to them about Galilean days. Though the kingdoms of his day challenged the King of all kingdoms, he preached the healing of the brokenhearted, the deliverance of the captives, the recovering of sight to the blind, the liberating of the bruised. He proclaimed but he also directed the proclamation to the discerned needs of the people. If this is life-situation preaching we should do more of it. The proclamation, however self-sufficient it may be, must pass through men who look round about on the people.

Certainly the message has changed since Christ came and lived among us, died in our stead, and rose in the power of God. Granted that no sermon wherever it begins, however it ends, is a Christian sermon unless Jesus Christ shines through it in one way or another; granted that we must proclaim Christ as well as Christ's proclamation; nevertheless, how did we work ourselves into that cul-de-sac which permits only the Petrine formula of preaching? How dare we say, as some do, that this Petrine formula is the only kind of New Testament preaching, cutting ourselves off from the possibility of preaching Christ in all the various ways in which Christ preached the Kingdom of God?

Yet that is what some theologians—the European particularly—would have us do. We have taken them too seriously; indeed, in this particular, they take themselves too seriously. Six or seven years ago the writer received from a friend, Dr. David Bryn-Jones, a copy of his little book *God's Grace and Man's Condition*. It contained, quite obviously, a series of sermons preached by Dr. Bryn-Jones to the students of International Christian University in Tokyo where he was serving in retirement as a professor. Biblically based, saturated with Christian doctrine, fashioned to enlighten and persuade, undergirded by the basic themes of the human and the divine drama, these were sermons, good ones—somewhat scholarly for the average congregation to be sure—but good sermons.

The preface of this little book was written by Dr. Emil Brunner, at that time Dr. Bryn-Jones's colleague. With a studied and pointed restraint Dr. Brunner referred to the sermons as "These addresses." And lest the slight should be missed he gratuitouly added the following explanation: "One critical remark I cannot, for the sake of honesty, suppress. We European theologians would not call these addresses 'sermons,' because we cannot, as many Americans seem to do, forget that what has been called preaching a sermon throughout all the centuries of Christian history has always been an exposition of a biblical text."[2] If we take only a casual glance at the record of Christian preaching through the centuries, we must say that Dr. Brunner's knowledge of the history of Christian preaching is spotty to say the least and that his "Christian history" omits the most important of all preaching ministries—that of Jesus Christ. What is important is not whether the sermon begins or ends with a text; there are good sermons, cherished by the church, which do neither. What matters is whether some needed word from God revealed in Jesus Christ is faithfully laid upon the hearts of the people.

What is it that makes a sermon relevant? Is it, as some ministers think, the use of a flippant, casual, sometimes vulgar language in the pulpit? Increasingly, though not yet generally, words from the tavern, the beatnik's pad, and the locker room find their way into the sermons of young ministers and old. The volume of such language, judging by the sermons submitted to *The Pulpit,* is not great as yet but some notes of caution may help prevent the development of an unfortunate trend. The use of vulgarities in the pulpit is defended on the ground that such language cuts through sham and pretense and comes to grips with reality. Earthly language, it is argued, has a vitality and a relevancy missing from accredited and acceptable vocabularies and is essential in communicating with the average parishioner today. If such language shocks, say the defenders of this position, if it offends the delicate sensitivities of the people, so what? How else can preaching shatter the people's protective shell of gentility?

It is instructive to note in any given sermon that the use of coarse slang is often in direct proportion to the minister's deficiency in the proper and effective handling of language. Offensive words are used inappropriately because the speaker does not know how to use correct words properly. Take, for example, one of the most frequent violations of good taste. To use the word *guts* when you mean intestines may in some instances be proper, although most dictionaries and most people now consider the word coarse. But to use this word as a neologism for courage is to betray ignorance of the myriad, forceful ways to convey the idea of bravery without resorting to ribald and repulsive slang. The use of linguistic rowdyisms in sermons, like the use of profanity, is frequently a substitute for intelligence.

At other times, however, intelligent ministers who have no language deficiency use the language of the street and speak publicly and graphically of the most distasteful shames of men's secret lives. They do so in order to prove their sophistication, to advertise their knowledge of, and by implication their ability to deal with, "the unfruitful works of darkness." A minister who wants to be a true pastor to his people will of course avoid a reputation as a prude who is detached from life and ignorant of the arenas in which the passions of men struggle. But if he is a pastor, diligently and conscientiously opening his life and his service to his people in the pastoral round, he will not have to use the pulpit to advertise his knowledge of human aberrations. He will not have to deal with the most sordid aspects of man's frailty and sin in the presence of the tender minds of children, the easily misdirected minds of adolescents, and the fixed gentilities of older people. Much is exposed to cleansing light in the study which need never be mentioned in the pulpit. Indeed, it is not only a perilous betrayal but also in the Apostle's words "a shame" even to speak in public of some things revealed in the confessional.

Moreover, ministers who are callously indifferent to the proprieties which their people expect the pulpit to observe and who in rare cases secretly enjoy shocking their flock with risqué hints and rustic allusions sometimes defend themselves on the ground that the gospel should offend the sensitivities of the people. No one who knows the cross of Jesus Christ will underestimate its power and its right to crush the inmost and most secure citadels of man's respectability. But obviously those ministers who defend their personal eccentricities by appealing to the gospel's offensiveness are indulging in a gross and blasphemous confusion of themselves with the gospel. The unvarnished gospel, purely and plainly preached, does offend the consciences of men; it does cut through their pride, their genteel morality, their protective manners, their smug reliance upon their own good breeding. But it is the gospel which should offend and not the minister or the grossness of the minister's vocabulary. There are manners and there is delicacy of taste which stand between a man and his Christ. No minister should let timidity or feigned modesty restrict his preaching of a gospel which breaks down this partition. But there are also manners and good taste, decorum and propriety, which are derivatives of the Gospel, which are not anti-Christ but Christly. To paraphrase the writer to the Romans: Do not for the sake of novelty, sophistication, and the bizarre destroy the work of God. Everything is indeed clean, but it is wrong for anyone to make others fall by what he speaks.

Note with what delicacy of touch and with what fine reserve the Apostle Paul in the First Letter to the Corinthians—a time and a people certainly no more prudish than we are now—wrote of certain parts of the body and of their functions: "On the contrary, the parts of the body which seem to be weaker are indispensable, and those parts of the body which we think less honorable we invest with the greater honor, and our unpresentable parts are treated with greater modesty, which our more presentable parts do not require" (I Cor. 12:22–24a). Paul was not a man of false modesty; he did not evade the precise word when the precise word alone would do. Nevertheless, he handled with prudence all public references to "our unpresentable parts." Ministers who are tempted to spice their sermons with ribaldry and gross frankness should refer to his example.

Do we make our preaching relevant by tailoring it ever so slightly, or, if necessary, drastically, to placate the whims and prejudices of the people? Some men think so. They say, "I must maintain communication with my people." Time and again this is the response of the minister who has been challenged to step out of his ministerial anonymity and the security of silence and champion some unconventional but plainly Christian position. The city hotels and restaurants do not accommodate Negroes; the local YMCA is showing "Operation Abolition"; an anti-Communism crusade is in town, dividing churches, smearing innocent reputations; the town fathers have repeatedly betrayed their trust; local union 74 is on strike and there is a bitter mood rising in the community. Someone should speak; someone with a respected voice should speak loud and clear; someone who can shed the light of the gospel or the compassion of the gospel or the judgment of the gospel should speak. But the minister of First Church is silent. Ask him about it and there are two chances out of three that in one way or another he will reply, "I must maintain communication with my people."

Disregard at once the respondents who are merely hypocritical in this reply. There are some, but not many. For these few the pat answer is an escape, a refuge, a dodge. There is a modicum of truth in it and they can rely upon that truth to conceal the true motivation of their silence and their inactivity. Dismiss also those who give this answer out of selfishness. They are more, but not many. They have a good thing in their churches and they know it and they are not about to let immoderate words or unconventional acts jeopardize their sinecures. Dismiss as well those who want to speak and act in Christ's name but are muted by fear. They are even more numerous, but still only a fraction of those who say, "I must maintain . . . etc." It isn't easy: If only we could preach as we should preach, live as a minister of Jesus Christ should live and—"get away with it." Why does duty so often come to us in the shape of a cross?

But of the many who say, "I must maintain communication with my people," what shall we say about those who have a pastor's big, warm heart, who sincerely dread nothing so much as estrangement from their people, who know that a shepherd can get so far ahead of the sheep that they no longer hear his voice—what about them?

It should be said first that few human relationships are quite so precious as that one which should and often does develop between a minister and the members of his church. The confidence of a congregation, so gratuitous and often so unmerited, must be handled as the sacred gift it is. None but the callous will treat it contemptuously; none but the prodigal will toss it away lightly.

Even so, who are "my people"? Is the minister's duty limited to those who belong to his church and pay its bills? Is he not also sent to "the lost sheep of the house of Israel," to the gentiles who ask only for the crumbs beneath the table? He may have a contract which binds him to some people, but he is under a covenant which binds him to all people. The poor, the brokenhearted, the captives, the blind, the bruised—must he not under that covenant maintain communication with *them*? They, too, whether in the church or out of it, are "my people."

Moreover, within the fellowship to which he is assigned, within the local congregation, "my people" will always include some—a remnant—who are receiving the ethical imperatives of Jesus Christ seriously, who are taking in the community and under Christ's bidding the hazardous step and are speaking the courageous word. They are trying in their faltering way to live out daily the ethical implications of the teaching and the spirit of Christ. They are venturing into areas of Christian witness and Christian service where the minister may be inactive and silent. Does not his dignified and calculated withdrawal break his communication with *them*? Willy-nilly, when the issues arise, he must break communication with someone; he cannot at all times be all things to all men. With whom shall he stand? With those who are earnestly seeking to do his Lord's will or with those who are saying merely "Lord, Lord"?

There comes to mind the increasing number of ministers who in the South are forced out of their pulpits or voluntarily resign because there has developed between pulpit and pew an intolerable conflict over the racial problem. There is a deep sadness here which no man can completely understand until it has happened to him. Nevertheless, this is not the worst thing that can happen to such ministers or to their churches. The worst thing that can happen to the ministers is an abdication of the duty they owe to God, and the worst thing that can happen to the churches is a pulpit which preserves in a sinful people a comfortable sense of guiltlessness. The racial question has created in many of our churches an agony which rises from the clashing of God's command that we love all men against the churches' racial divisions, their racial exclusiveness, and their unwillingness to take to their consciences the plight of the Negro in American society. Such agony is wholesome, or at least potentially wholesome. If the minister pampers the people with soothing words, with words which divert their eyes from their sins and from the Negroes' sorrows, the agony goes away. But it goes away without fulfilling its potential. Far better that the minister resign or be fired for laying the church's racial sins upon the hearts of the people than that he permit his desire for identity with his people to exorcise a guilt which only the people's repentance and obedience should remove.

There are times when the most appropriate things a minister can do for his people—and the last—is to sacrifice his relationship to them, doing so not in stubborn defiance but in humble obedience to his Lord. For the fact is that the minister's communication with his people is not the one thing necessary. What he should say is not "I must maintain my communication with my people" but "My people must maintain their communion with God and it is my role to help them do so." The times come—we can be grateful that they are rare—when the minister can maintain his communication with his people as a man of God only by breaking with them as a man among men. The time comes when he must stand over against them in judgment and in challenge if he would keep them for God rather than for himself. For their sakes and for God's sake he must be willing to live that life and speak that word which will lay God's claim upon them, even if the people repudiate him for doing so. See Amos, Jeremiah, Jesus.

The minister's yearning for communication and his desire to make what he says pertinent to the needs of his people may lead him into other equally fruitless detours. He is tempted to sprinkle the batter of his sermon with the spices of scientific, sociological, and psychological jargon—the very latest. This may give piquancy to his preaching and make it more palatable to a fastidious congregation, but it adds little nourishment. Or the minister is tempted to relate each sermon to the passing scene, letting the current news determine the subjects of his preaching rather than "the good news." No one knows the futility of such a procedure better than the editor of a journal of contemporary preaching. Required to select sermons for publication three and four months in advance, he pays scant attention to sermons which deal with the Eichmann case or Oxford, Mississippi, or the latest proposal for church union unless the sermon uses the current event to uncover and apply the timeless truth. Otherwise, what is contemporary when he receives it is dated and irrelevant when it is published. To be sure, the minister in the local parish does not work under this kind of schedule, but if he rivets his preaching consistently to the passing scene, soon or late he is preaching not to the present and to the future but to the past. If he preaches the eternal, illustrating that preaching with the current, he will always be contemporary. Or, once more, the minister in his hunger for relevancy may fall into a "preaching" which echoes the whims of the people in Christian terminology, telling them only what they want to hear. Considering the variety of ways in which we ministers can go wrong in our search for relevancy, it is not surprising that a movement should rise against this search.

What is the right way to achieve relevancy in our preaching? To answer this question we must note at least three requisites of the good sermon, moving from the least to the most important. A good preacher must be a craftsman, a pastor, and, in something more than the social reformer sense of the word, a prophet.

We need not repeat here what many excellent books on sermon preparation have already said about craftsmanship. We do need to pause long enough for a confession before we move on to more important matters. All of us must grant that too many of our sermons are amoeboid, pools of literary protoplasm flowing in all directions at once. Too many of them are cluttered with lumbering, ponderous sentences: subclauses added to secondary clauses added to subordinate clauses until no one, including the speaker, knows what is actually being said. Or, on the other hand, many of our sermons, when we try to give them shape, become gaunt and skeletal, all bones and no flesh. Correcting these deficiencies means work; for most of us it means hard work, the labor through which passion entrusts its power to style.

The skillful homiletician will not be interested in style for style's sake. He will know instinctively or he will have learned that when the style of the sermon is made an end in itself, the sermon becomes affected, self-conscious, and mechanical. He preaches a gospel, not a style. He knows that artificial embellishments which give glitter and polish to a sermon will also inevitably sheathe its cutting edge. However, when we speak of homiletical style we are not thinking of adornments. "Style," as J. Middleton Murry said, "is organic, not the clothes a man wears, but the flesh, blood and bone of his body." The idea of the sermon must find a form—its own organic form—or remain an invisible, inaudible, secret abstraction. If the language misleads, deceives, confuses, or proves inadequate, then the idea, the sermonic proposal, dies in transmission, however virile it may be.

The truthfulness and the veracity of the sermon are tested by the style of the sermon. Coleridge insisted on "the importance of accuracy of style as being near akin to veracity and truthful habits of mind; he who thinks loosely will write loosely." The corollary for ministers is that he who preaches loosely has thought loosely. If the homiletical idea refuses to emerge in plain, vital, intelligible form, the minister must conclude either that the idea is not valid and worthy of the pulpit or that he has not given it the time, the skill, and the exploration it deserves.

Moreover, the sacredness of the sermonic idea deserves excellent style and is defamed if we do not grant to that idea the finest structure we are able to give it. If it is worth preaching, it is worth preaching well. To write carelessly, to speak carelessly, is to imply that the thoughts being conveyed are not really very important after all. "Rightly handling the word of truth" requires neither unctuous tones nor ornate phrases, but it does require that we put all our talents at the disposal of the gospel. We can do this and still "be natural, be simple, be yourself: shun artifices, tricks, fashions."

Again, communication demands good style. Religious art has been defined as the successful communication of a valuable religious experience. The sermon is one form of that art; an effective sermon is a successful communication of a valuable religious experience through the spoken word. The minister must therefore make himself the master of that language which promotes the flow, the impact, the penetration and the reception of ideas. A sermon is not a soliloquy accidentally overheard by a congregation. It is not a monologue which can arrogantly say to the listeners, "Find out what I mean if you can." A sermon is a dialogue. The spoken part of this sermonic dialogue—if in this area we may take advice from Schopenhauer—must be especially clear precisely because the speaker cannot hear the unspoken part of the dialogue which takes place within the mind of the listener. The success of the sermon depends not only upon the adequacy of the listener but also upon the clarity, the winsomeness, and the power of that form in which the sermon emerges. If the minister is determined that there shall be such a dialogue, that meaning shall be conveyed and received through his sermon, his style will begin to take care of itself.

Secondly, an effective preacher must be a pastor as well as a craftsman. George Buttrick put it categorically: "Only the pastor, or a man with pastoral imagination, can preach."[3] To ask what a pastor is may appear naïve, yet there are few professional titles which are as blurred as this one. Ask the average minister what a pastor is and he will tell you what a pastor *does*: house-to-house visitations in the parish; special ministries to the sick, the dying, and the bereaved; person-to-person encounters in counseling sessions; the solemnizing of weddings, funerals, and dedications. Ask him *why* he does these things, what purposes confer authority and validity to the minister's pastoral role, what transcending design catches and orders his counseling and calling, praying and pleading, consoling and challenging, and he will be hard put to answer. He plays the role because this is what ministers do, but the average minister can give at best only a fuzzy definition of the overarching meaning and purpose of his pastoral service.

Ask the average member of the average congregation what a pastor is and the picture he draws will be none too flattering. It will be a bland composite which shows the pastor as the congregation's congenial, ever helpful, ever ready to help boy scout; as the darling of the old ladies and as sufficiently reserved with the young ones; as the father image for the young people and a companion to lonely men; as the affable glad-hander at teas and civic club luncheons. The exciting and intriguing colors which should go into a portrait of a pastor have either been omitted or have faded until what is left is the image of an innocuous, well-meaning, but drab and ineffective fellow.

This popular image of the pastor convinces many devoted young men that they can perform a more meaningful Christian service outside of the professional ministry than they can in it; and this image, far more than the declining social and professional status of the minister, aggravates the enrollment problem which currently confronts most Protestant seminaries. Moreover, this view of the pastoral role is driving hundreds of young seminarians away from the parish ministry into specialized ministerial services: teaching, the chaplaincy, inner-city mission work, social service. Such posts deserve their share of the available talent, but seminarians should not be driven into such specialized services by a repugnant view of the pastorate.

What image of the pastor did George Buttrick have in mind when he made pastoral imagination essential to good preaching? Probably he was thinking in biblical terms and of the original and basic meaning of the word *pastor*. The biblical view of the pastor and the current one are in sharpest possible contrast. In the noun form the biblical word means a *shepherd*; and to the ancient mind that word implied courage, concern, patience, care, and an intense sensitivity on the part of the shepherd to the collective and personal needs of the sheep. The shepherd's role in the ancient world—and presently in some lands—was an arduous one but there was glamour in it; it was lonely but there was mystery and romance in it;

it was lowly but there was dignity in it. In the verb form the biblical word *pastor* means "to tend a flock, to rule, to nourish." Perhaps we should not take "to rule" too seriously in this day when "Herr Pastor" has disappeared in all but the most secluded Lutheran communities of our land; but "to tend" and "to nourish" apply.

And what an astounding genealogy this word has. Chronologically in biblical history the word *pastor* is applied first to God: "The Lord is my shepherd" (Ps. 23:1b"). It is applied second to Christ: "I am the good shepherd; I know my own and my own know me, as the Father knows me and I know the Father; and I lay down my life for the sheep" (John 10:14–15). It is applied third to Christ's ministers: "And his gifts were that some should be apostles, some prophets, some evangelists, some pastors and teachers, for the equipment of the saints, for the work of ministry, for building up the body of Christ, until we all attain to the unity of the faith and of the knowledge of the Son of God, to mature manhood, to the measure of the stature of the fulness of Christ" (Eph. 4:11–13). The pastor wears a title worn first by God and then by Christ and then only by Christ's minister. It is difficult to conceive of a higher professional aristocracy.

The minister, however, is not always worthy of the title. In *Lycidas* Milton used strange words to describe unworthy pastors. He called them "blind mouths." In commenting on this phrase Ruskin said that this is not a broken metaphor but a pithy description of the exact "contraries of right character, in the two great offices of the church—those of bishop and pastor. A bishop means a person who sees. A pastor means one who feeds. The most unbishoply character a man can have is therefore to be blind. The most unpastoral is, instead of feeding, to want to be fed—to be a mouth."[4] So the pastor is one who tends and feeds, who nourishes men with Christ, and with a shepherd's watchful eye tries to keep men in Christ's fold.

In the process he lays down his life for his sheep. Indeed? No, in this day not often in deed does a pastor lay down his life for his people—although now and then, here and there, it does happen. But he dies for the sheep in the sense that he is always entering in spirit into the lives of other men. This is what the true pastor means by that word *empathy* which has become so popular with him in recent years: he has an extraordinary sensitivity to the yearnings and fears of the people; he projects his own consciousness into other human beings and is willing to absorb into his own being whatever he finds there—agony or joy, wretchedness or glory. He can "rejoice with those who rejoice, weep with those who weep." Anyone who has tried it knows that this requires a dying unto oneself.

Such thoughts drift easily over the line between the solemn and the maudlin, but the pastor cannot be defined without saying about him what the scriptures say. And this is what the scriptures say: the pastor is one who lays down his life for the sheep. A certain seminary president used to remind the students in periodic chapel talks that, though their salaries would be small in the pastorate, there would be priceless compensations which would not have the ring of cash. There are; and one of them is the joy of dying for other men so that they may live. The true pastor knows this joy. Santa Teresa's enigmatic saying is not paradoxical to him: "I die because I am not dying." The Master's word does not puzzle him: "For whoever would save his life will lose it; and whoever loses his life for my sake will find it" (Matt. 16:25). There is a beautiful Spanish word for which there is no English equivalent. The word is *agonizante*—one who assists a dying person and shares his agony. The true pastor is *agonizante*.

By his dictum George Buttrick meant in part that "though a true sermon may be in measure true anywhere, it is most centrally and sharply true in the congregation for whom it is prepared." Thus he implies that the pastor is the temporal coagulant calling the congregation into being. He is in the midst of the people as the visible reminder of the judgment and the love of God in Jesus Christ. For a moment change the figure from the sheepfold to the apiary. In Maeterlinck's enchanting *The Life of the Bee* the author remarks upon the honeybee's need for community: "She will dive for an instant into flower-filled space, as the swimmer will dive into the sea that is filled with pearls, but under pain of death it behooves her at regular intervals to return and breathe the crowd as the swimmer must return and breathe the air. Isolate her, and however abundant the food or favorable the temperature, she will expire in a few days not of hunger or cold, but of loneliness."[5] This is a way of saying that you cannot keep *a* bee; you can keep only bees. Nor can you keep *a* Christian; you can keep only Christians. Perhaps it is true that outside of the church there is no salvation.

At Iowa State University one of the world's leading bee experts, when asked whether Maeterlinck's poetic description is factual, replied that bee scientists now suspect that there is a social hormone which the queen bee secretes and which is passed through the hive by the worker bees which cluster around the queen. Without the hormone of community the hive dies. The hormone of the Christian community is the Holy Spirit, and the pastor is the chief of the workers who are visible reminders that this mysterious and indispensable cohesive is passing through the hive. Half in jest Fosdick once said that in the Protestant tradition the minister is a necessary evil. Evil, not necessarily; necessary, yes.

How often the people say that they do not want to be preached at. By *at* they mean, among other things, the preaching of a man who is detached from them by an unpastoral busyness with other things, who measures his importance by the number of times and the distance he travels from the parish or who lets his own trials and sorrows estrange him from "the sore and stricken hearts of his fellowmen." By *at* they mean preaching which is intellectually immaculate but which is devoid of all compassionate warmth, preaching which is academically and theologically correct but which is not recognized by the people as the truth which rises within them even as it enters through their ears. By *at* they mean the preaching of a man who, living among them, remains a stranger to the passions, the trials, and the twisted hopes as well as to the little joys and the big victories which make up their lives. By *at* they mean a man whose sympathetic nerves, over which the people's pains and pleasures should creep, are benumbed. By *at* they mean the preaching of a man who is not a pastor.

What are the transcending purposes which give meaning to the sometimes dreary and wearisome pastoral round? The letter to the Ephesians suggests the answer: "And his gifts were that some should be . . . pastors . . . for the equipment of the saints, for the work of ministry, for building up the body of Christ . . ." (Eph. 4:11-12). The true pastor will help his people, his "saints," celebrate life, teaching them the sacramental significance of household tasks, of the ordinary personal encounters, of the bread-earning jobs. He will awaken in them the vision which sees that every bush is aflame and arouse or cultivate in them joy in the poetry which is concealed in the prosaic. He will urge upon them the thrill of being "faithful in a very little," which may prove to be their only warranty that they are "faithful also in much." Stefan Zweig said of Dickens, "He gave to simple things and unpretentious people a glory all their own. . . . To thousands, nay to millions, he revealed where to find the everlasting spark in their uneventful lives, where to look for the glow of quiet joy beneath the ashes of the familiar."[6] If the minister's influence does not fall upon his people with something of this same effect, he is no pastor.

He will not be able to bring this off merely by exhibiting a sunny disposition. The times are too somber for that. He must find a more permanent, a more primordial fixed ground for the celebration of life under the shadow of death. He himself must go back repeatedly to the God who made life and called it good, who lets man be beset by adversities, and who ordered the earning of bread by the sweat of the brow. Some bread-earning jobs to be sure are humiliating. And Christians whose burdens allow them no other alternative but to go on with such jobs need the pastor's help in bringing cheer into a monotonous life. God has approved life, struggle, and labor; we cannot despise them as though they were alien to his will. The pastor must return his people to the God who "set the solitary in families" and who, when he appeared on earth, came not from the sky but into a family. The loss of family life, of the joys of family life, is a repudiation of the God who crowned the home prior to the church and the state.

Seeking a ground on which he and his people can solemnize life, the pastor must sit and must set his people at the feet of those acts through which Jesus Christ vindicated the common ventures of life in the midst of world-shaking and world-destroying events. Rome was strangling in the convolutions of its own gore and lust; stiff-necked Jerusalem was inviting its own destruction; the plight of the outcasts of the house of Israel was still unrelieved; yet in the midst of these great occasions the Son of man turned to salute the uneventful experiences of life and to grace the domestic duties by his own obedience. As the Book of Common Prayer has it, matrimony's "holy estate Christ adorned and beautified with his presence and first miracle that he wrought in Cana of Galilee." He found time for conversation with friends in the home of Martha, Mary, and Lazarus. He expressed a child's wondering joy in simple things: in flowers, leaven, seed, and a cup of cold water. He saw unconscious meaning in the simple act of the woman who cooled and soothed his feet with ointment. And in his last act he provided for his widowed mother.

Thus Christ stamped the seal of God upon the wearisome routine; fitted our general, everyday experiences into the cosmic scheme; sanctified the debts which human beings owe to one another. It was his way of saying that the hinged events on which the epochs turn and empires rise and kingdoms fall have no more merit in God's sight and no higher place in his plan than the common ties of duty and service and pleasure which weave together the family of man. The pastor as preacher and the preacher as pastor will equip the saints with a redeeming sense of the sacramental quality of life.

Following the rubric given in the letter to the Ephesians, it is the duty of the pastor to prepare the people "for the work of ministry." To call all men to the ministry of Jesus Christ may be primarily a preaching function; to prepare them for that ministry is primarily a pastoral function. Therefore, the true pastor-preacher leads his people not only into a commemoration of the sacramental aspect of the common life but also into a commemoration of the sacramental quality of their own lives in the service of Jesus Christ. Indeed they cannot do the first without also doing the second. They, too, cannot live unless daily they are dying unto Christ. This is not a rule written for religious specialists. It is a rule by which the whole fabric of all human life is watermarked. The pastor-preacher is not imposing on his people when he calls them to, and prepares them for, a life which is spent as the sacrament through which God blesses other men. On the contrary, he does them the greatest disservice when he mutes this claim which Christ has on all his disciples. And the disservice is compounded if the preacher calls them and the pastor does not prepare them.

And, once more, we are pastors "for building up the body of Christ." We are engaged as pastors not only in helping our people to celebrate the sacraments of the common life, not only in leading them and preparing them to commit their lives to Christ as living sacraments, but also we are under orders to lead the whole people in the building of the church, in the administering of the sacrament of Christian community. By "the church" we mean here the koinonia, the fellowship, the community of God's gathered people. Let the promoter and the administrator and the chairman of the finance committee build that external and visible church which may or may not have anything to do with the body of Christ. God builds up the body of Christ and the pastor is one of his instruments. But in this enterprise the people have a say; they can make it or break it. How often it is that harassed men, chased through all the avenues and dark alleys of life, flee to the church and find that it, too, is no sanctuary. They find a club, a stratum of society, a symbol of respectability, but no sanctuary. Pastors are not appointed for building up any of these but are appointed "for building up the body of Christ."

Such a man may not necessarily preach a good sermon; something more must be added to the definition of significant and effective preaching. But relevant preaching comes to the people only through such a man. He need not be the stated and employed minister of a local church; Paul was a free-lance preacher; but his apostleship nevertheless had its pastoral qualities. But in the larger sense we must accept Buttrick's dictum: "Only the pastor, or a man with pastoral imagination, can preach."

Last, but most important, no preaching is appropriate to the times and pertinent to the needs of the people unless it is prophetic. What then do we mean by prophetic preaching? In one of his writings Thomas Chalmers said, "A moderate sermon is like a winter's day, short and clear and cold. The brevity is good; the clarity is better; the coldness is fatal." This, more than anything else, is the radical defect of contemporary preachings: the sermons are moderate; they are cold. The thunder and lightning of God's "No!" is not in them; the warmth and the light of God's "Yes!" is dimmed. Our sermons too seldom tug at those chains which bind man to the earth or show those hands which free him and lift him into heaven. The themes are not deep, grand, and timeless but pretty and ephemeral; the treatment is routine; the language is pedestrian. But note that coldness is not the lack of sentimental feelings or romantic language; coldness is the absence of energy, of movement. At absolute zero—some sermons approach it—there is absolute immobility. This sermonic inertness cannot be corrected by craftsmanship. If the sermons are cold, this is so because they are dead; and if they are dead, they cannot be warmed into life by the incorporation of human-interest stories and sentimental illustrations. A more radical resurrection is required.

"Clergymen are numerous," said Charles E. Jefferson, "but prophets are few."[7] This line from a recent anthology, *The Best of Charles E. Jefferson,* is a just and accurate indictment of current preaching. With one incisive stroke it uncovers the weakness underlying the decadence of the American pulpit. By the word *prophets* Jefferson did not mean social reformers; in fact, he insisted that a man who is solely a pulpit reformer "does not wear his crown long." He was referring rather to men who with conviction and passion and in truth hopefully speak for the God of Peril and Promise, whose pulpits remind men, not of the lecturer's dais or the forum or a cozy experiment in group dynamics, but of Sinai, Calvary, and the Areopagus.

Historically, the prophet is one who stands in an intimate relationship to the history of his own time, but his message is directed not to the superficial waves of his time but to the deep Gulf Streams which flow beneath the surface of life. He sees as others do not the dominant and decisive trends and the immediate and ultimate outcome of those trends. Historians can interpret historical events after they happen. Prophets understand the trends of the times while they are happening. To study the prophets of old is not to explore the antiquities but to discover the eternities. In doing so we do not exhume what has been long dead but unveil what is forever living. The archaeologists dig into the past to discover what was; when we study the prophets we are digging into the past to discover what is. The prophets always have about them not the smell of death but of life.

In his own limited way, granting that he cannot be an Amos or a Jeremiah, every preacher must be a prophet. That is, he speaks of temporal things in their eternal terms. And though he may be no immortal seer, his limitations are not so great as might be supposed. For God instructs the listening prophet in the invariable nature of the Peril and the varieties of its assaults and in the reality and the certainty and the finality of the Promise. He is not reduced to dull abstractions and vague suppositions. In his preaching he names places and events and speaks a current tongue. But he speaks to unfolding history from a point of fixed reference beyond history. He knows what God has said and through him is saying. He is intensely concerned about the general and the particular human experience, but he brings to that experience not the word which is trivial, external, and passing but the one which abides. In doing this he is not limited to Bible and to doctrine but Bible and doctrine are always the safest and the surest place to begin.

So, whatever else may be missing from our preaching, the major deficiency is that spiritual passion which comes from the knowledge that we are dealing with ultimate and elemental things. When we speak of "spiritual passion" we are referring, of course, not to the simulated earnestness and the feigned enthusiasm which can be adopted and projected by an artful actor but to that passion which consumes the minister when God grips him with a Word to speak and the compulsion to speak it. And when we speak of "ultimate and elemental things" we are referring to the issues of life and death, blessing and curse, Promise and Peril. The line from Charles E. Jefferson which scores the tameness, the superficiality, and the ambivalence of much of our preaching comes from a book which in its design serves as a parable. It is a parable which declares the difference between prophetic preaching and other forms of public address. The first half of the book is devoted to sermons; the second half to conversations. This division and the contrast between the sermons and the conversations are a corrective to which preachers should pay close attention. The conversations deal in the main with themes which are pertinent and timely but whose importance is at best penultimate. They are prudential moralities on such themes as thoughtfulness, patience, contentment; practical instructions to lay-men, ministers, ministers' wives; and quiet talks for family settings. No one reading them would question the value of such discourses or their art, skill, and winsomeness. But they are not sermons; they are pious and pleasant talks on familiar themes.

When we turn to Jefferson's sermons, we find ourselves in a different realm. The contrast between what he said in the pulpit and what he said in other settings is striking and conclusive. The subjects of the sermons are also pertinent and practical; they address man, as he is and where he is; but they bring to him something more than man's word to man. The difference is that the themes of the sermons are not only timely and practical but also timeless and ultimate; they are magnificent subjects magnificently developed: God, the Bible, the continuous yearning of the soul for its Redeemer, eternal life, the divine demand for social vision and justice. To be sure, Jefferson did not wander aimlessly over the broad scope of each of these subjects. His selectivity and his emphasis brought each message to a cutting edge which stirred the conscience and moved the will; nevertheless, all that he had to say in each of these sermons had direct rootage in some cardinal declaration of the gospel and had application to the real issues of life.

If a doctor, arriving at the scene of an accident, knows that he has only twenty minutes at most in which to save a victim's life, he will waste none of them combing the patient's hair or brushing his clothes, or checking marks of identification. He will move as swiftly as he can to the most critical and threatening wound and will address to it all his skills and supplies. He deals immediately with the most serious threat to life. Something similar is demanded of the minister in the pulpit. He has his twenty minutes, more or less, in which to bring life to someone within his hearing or in which to let him die. There is no time for the tea and cookies of amiable conversation. The pulpit is neither the social nor the sports nor the comic pages of the newspaper; it is the lost-and-found column which lists those items that have to do with man's soul and his community. This, put another way, is the meaning of the plea for a return to biblical and doctrinal preaching. Our Protestant fathers bounded the sermon with a definition which excludes from the pulpit the merely conversational themes: "Doctrines must be preached practically, and duties doctrinally." Any sermon which does not find itself at home somewhere within this ample definition is simply not a sermon.

The fundamental question about the relevancy of our preaching has to do with its genuineness rather than with its contemporaneity.

Does it deal with the essential stuff of human nature and the human experience? Are there sounds in it as primitive and as elemental as a baby's cry, food in it as basic as bread, vistas in it which open all the way to God's throne? None of this will be said better than J. H. Jowett put it sixty years ago: "Do we impress the people with the feeling that we are dealing with trifles, or with blinding and appalling enormities? . . . If sin has become a commonplace, our preaching has become a plaything. If we do not feel its horrors, we shall lose the startling clarion of the watchman. There will be no urgency in our speech, no vehemence, no sense of imperious haste. If we think lightly of the disease, we shall loiter on the way to the physician."[8] Or to put the thought finally in our own words, does the scalpel of our preaching cut through the subcutaneous layers of our people's consciences or does it lie limp and light on the surface? Does it grasp the realness and the earnestness and the innerness of human existence and does it to this existence bring a warning and a hope and a way which are something more than man's cheery encouragement to man? Is God in it, and the devil, and the Christ? Is the Peril in it, and the Promise, and the Cross?

Make your preaching in this sense genuine and you will have no difficulty making it relevant. More than a hundred years ago it was said, in a comment on the preaching of C. H. Spurgeon, "A preacher is not divinely called and elevated to be a facile weathercock, turned by the wind; but, like a tower of strength in scenes of danger, not less luminous than resolute, he is to turn the winds."[9] It is a big job, but there is no one of us who cannot by the grace of God perform it successfully.

4

Recovering the Preacher's Identity

Diagnostic studies of the Protestant minister in recent years have consistently concluded that the minister's chief sickness is a loss of professional particularity. His office divides not only into its elemental parts—pastor, preacher, priest—but also into various additional duties which are only tenuously related to his calling. Like the Nile, the river of his ministry disintegrates, loses its thrust, and disappears in multiple streamlets. There has been little disposition on the part of the clergy to dispute this diagnosis. Ministers insist that there are exceptions—and surely there are many—but they admit that the average minister is a victim of vocational amnesia: he does not know who he is. The studies which point to this conclusion range from the restrained, dispassionate scholarship of H. Richard Niebuhr and his collegues in *The Purpose of the Church and Its Ministry* to Joseph Sittler's intriguing description of the clergy's malaise as "the maceration of the minister." Uniformly the analyses point to the fragmentation of the ministerial profession and the minister's consequent loss of professional identity.

This lack of professional identity has caused the clergy to dabble in many things in church and society blithely hoping that some mystic and invisible cord will somehow pull all these scattered func-

tions into one significant purpose consistent with the minister's calling. The results are several, the first of which is the ministerial
accent on amiability. Large segments of the clergy have made a
fetish, bordering on heresy, out of Paul's "all things to all men."
Paul had in mind the need of Christ's representatives for what we
call empathy, a sensitivity to the varieties of human nature and of
human need and the ability to enter imaginatively and sympatheti-
cally into those varieties. What the ever-amiable minister often has
in mind is something quite different. Too often his amiability
expresses a hunger to be everywhere favorably received, to be the
beloved member of church and community. This may not be and
often is not a crass selfishness on the minister's part; it may express
a compassion for all men. Nevertheless, the desire to have all men's
approval can be deadly. All of us can think of ministers who by
their loveableness and their trustworthiness have inspired and com-
forted us. We are grateful for them, but if the minister purchases
that image at the expense of the gospel, if he is lured into speaking
pleasant words on all occasions and to all people to preserve that
image, he may remain acceptable to the people but he is no longer
pleasing to God. God requires that his will be declared whether
or not it pleases the people and whether or not its declaration makes
the minister favorable in the eyes of the people. When F. L.
Anderson came in his youth to be the minister of the Second Baptist Church in Rochester, New York, an elderly lady said to him
after his first sermon, "How can you, young as you are, expect to
please seven hundred people?" To this question Anderson gave an
answer which could be misconstrued as sanctimonious but which
is the only answer a minister should give to such a question. He
said, "I did not come here to please seven hundred people: I came
to please One." He knew whose he was. He became a beloved
minister but this was an incidental development.

A second and kindred result of the loss of professional identity is that the minister in his preaching and his pastoral duties resorts to sentimentality. In Daniel Jenkins' definition ministers begin to think of themselves not as servants of Jesus Christ but "as 'big brothers' who exist to prove 'helping hands' and to diffuse 'radiant cheerfulness' to their people." Most ministers have not, as Jenkins charges, explicitly denied that their duty is to proclaim the Word of God to all men in all their conditions as that Word is revealed in Jesus Christ. What they have done in their resort to sentimentality is to extract from the gospel those words which speak of the Promise and from that extraction have distilled a soothing balm which has little reference to man's Peril and scant resemblance to God's Promise.

A third result is the ministerial addiction to activity. Now and then there does appear in the ministry that genius who is accomplished and competent in more than one field; but who is qualified to be all things expected of a minister: humorist, administrator, civic leader, politician, writer, reformer, preacher, shepherd, priest? Yet thousands of ministers with a reckless gallantry which says more for their valor than for their discretion accept the challenge of this multiple assignment. Like an harassed genie the average minister adopts so many forms that he no longer remembers which is his true one. He is heavy on action and light on motivation.

This addiction to activity is particularly tempting to the minister in the area of social reformation. When the world is as now so much out of joint, the sensitive and alert soul is exceedingly vulnerable to the suggestion that it was born to set the world right. Not so long ago a seminary president made to ministers and to seminary students the astounding proposal that "before the answer to the questions of war and poverty are found, some of us may have to quit the pulpit for the soapbox, the parish house for the barracks

and the church for the labor-forum."[1] It must be said to his credit
that he had the good sense to ignore his own bizarre advice and
ended his illustrious career in the parish ministry. But such a statement from such a position indicates how far the clergy sometimes
wanders from any unique, to say nothing of divine, purpose. The
pull of the world's needs is strong on us and it should be; to neglect
those needs is to disown the God who "so loved the world." But
the clergy's primary and pre-emptive mission is not to be the cus-
todian of a culture or the architects of a better world. Ministers are
not sent to be the lackeys of every good cause, signatories of excellent resolutions and worthy petitions, or even primarily to be cham-
pions of justice. They are sent to speak for that Christ who is
sovereign over man's whole psychic and social realm.

To be sure, this message in all its varied implications must be
freshly related to the real needs of each succeeding and different
day. On one side there is the danger of that pietism which secludes
itself from the affairs of this world and "gives way to monastic
gout." Toward that danger the critics of any social expression of
the gospel would lure the ministry by cajolery or drive it by intimi-
dation. But there is another danger much more tempting than
monastic gout, and that is St. Vitus' dance—external spasms and
twitchings but no central control, no one-directional motivation.
It is one thing for the minister to have all the world come to his
private dwelling, importuning his attention, his allegiance, his sup-
port. It is quite another thing to go to all the world, into every
nook and corner of its multiple affairs, with the witness to a God
whose love and judgment, justice and mercy and infallible will,
shine through the face of Jesus Christ. The minister is called into
a service in which more often than not there is a complete reversal
of the human expectation, in which the men who do the most good
for this world are often those whose hearts are riveted to another

world, in which only that word which is eternal is ever properly temporal, and in which a life lived out in obscure, self-forgetting service may shape man's future as no popular idol can. It was said of Benedict of Nursia "that he never dreamt of regenerating anything but his own soul and those of his brethren, the monks." Yet the beneficial impact of this life upon the flow of European civilization has so many ramifications that it is immeasurable. It could well be that the most practical question a minister can ask himself today is not the social or professional one but that question which searches the depths of his own character and dedication.

The fourth result of the minister's lack of professional identity is that he surrenders himself to the wrong authority. In *From State Church to Pluralism* Franklin Hamlin Littell suggests that the prophetic message is sometimes killed by "the vulgar control of pulpits." Let us presume that he is referring not to bishops and district superintendents but to the bold, crass effort of some laymen to dominate the pulpit with their own views by harassing and intimidating the minister. To illustrate this point—which is certainly not news to any minister who has in any way condemned the status quo in the name of Jesus Christ—Littell quotes a statement which a leading citizen of Georgia made in the Emory University *Alumnus*: " . . . if their advocacy from their pulpits (in which they are, in the last analysis, the paid guest speakers) becomes sufficiently obnoxious to their listeners to cause a substantial decline in attendance and gross receipts . . . the clergyman mustn't be too surprised when the church fathers arrange for his transfer to more favorable climes."[2]

In every church there is a nub of laymen who believe what the Emory University alumnus put in crass but admirably frank words. To them the minister is a hireling, a paid guest speaker, whose business it is, not to declare from the pulpit the often offensive judgments and the sometimes humiliating mercies of God but to echo instead the mind and the mood of the people. Such laymen go further, indeed. Not only do they believe that the voice of the people is the voice of God; they believe that *they* are the voice of the people. There is nothing democratic about their insistence that the minister preach what the people want preached. On the contrary, by such insistence they try to put under their "vulgar control" both the pulpit and the people. When the minister stands his ground and insists that the pulpit remain unbound, he is often pleasantly surprised to discover that *they* are not the people.

That some people speak of their minister (they stress the possessive pronoun) as though he were merely an employee, that many think it and some act upon it, it is neither surprising nor the worst thing that can happen to the minister. The worst thing is that he should come to think of himself in such terms. If he lets timidity, cupidity, or amiability force him into the role of "paid guest speaker," canceling what God has made him and called him to be, he profanes the pulpit and smears his vocation. But the pulpit will not be sullied by the people's image of the minister if the minister refuses to accept the image. On the contrary, the people will respect his high calling in Jesus Christ if he respects it himself.

Although the loss of ministerial identity is sufficiently general to be called epidemic, the minister's reactions to it are varied and fall mainly into four patterns. The first pattern, which like the rest cannot be statistically documented, includes those ministers who are fully aware of the problem, who have seen themselves sinking into it, but who in one way or the other have solved it, at least to their own satisfaction. This category is not big enough to contain all of the ministers who believe that they belong in it, but those who do belong in this classification do not need the corrections which are suggested here.

The second pattern includes that small group of clergymen who find the minister's dilemma so insufferable and so insoluble that they withdraw either temporarily or permanently from the parish ministry. The most dramatic incident in this category occurred in the late summer of 1962 when Dr. Lowell Russell Ditzen, for twelve years the successful and beloved minister of The Reformed Church of Bronxville, New York, resigned. This church, with its thirty-four hundred members served by five ministers, is one of the great churches of America, according to any of the tapes by which we usually take such measurements. If Dr. Ditzen had been moving to some other church or to a denominational office, or if a disagreement had developed between him and the church, his resignation would not have been unusual; but this was not the case. He resigned under no external pressure and without immediate personal plans for the future. In a pastoral letter he explained his seemingly peculiar action to the members of the congregation: "It can be put in one sentence: I am convinced it is God's will. First, as a minister I am committed to the way of spiritual and intellectual growth. Only so can I, or any clergyman, adequately fulfill his role of spiritual guide. Now in the church that has grown about us, numbering some thirty-four hundred souls, with the ever-increasing administrative demands and calls for a personal ministry to people with wide-varied problems, the first matter is increasingly pushed in the background. I would not be fair to my calling or to you to continue a program that progressively prohibits my doing 'first things.'

"Secondly, I am aware that our generation is facing more ominous days than when I completed my graduate studies twenty-five years ago. Our great Protestant churches are not fulfilling, with power and light, their roles. Why? One reason is that clergymen, like myself, have become bound by the web of 'programs and mechanics,' till they have no time to be quiet and hear 'the still small voice.' . . .

"Thirdly, I am deeply concerned about our nation. America has a destiny in history. Yet our religious trumpets are giving an uncertain sound. America and Americans are not being called to the high road of personal responsibility, integrity and vision on which we should be walking. Again, why? Because religious leaders, like myself, do not have the time to drink from the fountains of our origin, to study the real issues of the present and so to inspire us to greatness by prophetic utterance. I do not say I will find the answers. I only know I must try."

The third pattern includes the many ministers who may want to follow Ditzen's example, who may be as eager as he was to close the door on the multiplying ministerial roles once and for all and go to some Arabia in search of that one role which gives a self-recognized, respectable, and satisfying identity to the minister, but who cannot cut the Gordian knot as he did. For one practical reason or another, or because the alternative he chose has for them no appeal, these ministers must work out the problem where they are. And they work at it; they are not resigned to spending the balance of their ministry in activated desperation, flying from one thing to another. Caught in the ecclesiastical machine they rebel against the machine; but in the end and for most ministers the machine wins. Most of the ministers who are conscious of what is happening to them, who periodically resolve to break out of the moving box in which they are caught, nevertheless end their ministries echoing the plaintive cry of one of Shakespeare's characters, "Who is it that can tell me who I am?"

The fourth pattern describing the reaction of ministers to the problem of professional fragmentation includes—we may safely assume—a much larger group of ministers and describes an even more serious aspect of the problem. Some ministers, even though they exhibit all the symptoms of the clerical disease, are blithely unaware of the fact that they are sick. Indeed, they count the symptoms of disease—their busyness, their exciting diversity of duties, their multiplied roles—as signs of health. The fact that the building program, the financial campaign, the civic club's agenda, the church suppers, the schedule for the athletic teams, as well as the pastoral-preaching-priestly function all depend upon them they accept as a tribute to their worthiness and proof of their indispensability. Despite what some analysts assume, the extraministerial offices which the church, community, and denominational headquarters thrust upon these ministers are not ordeals which the ministers accept reluctantly and which against their will shatter their professional purpose into multifarious purposes. On the contrary, for many ministers such diversified activities are enticing detours, welcomed escapes from the monotony of the study and the wearisome routine of the pastoral round.

The fact of the matter is directly contrary to those sentimental defenses of the "overburdened" minister which appear occasionally in popular journals. In far more cases than would admit it, the minister is overburdened because he wants to be overburdened. He wears many hats in church and community because the multiple roles they represent constitute his only identity, his image of himself. This man's name is Legion; his sense of integrity is dependent not upon his being one thing but precisely upon his being many things. His ministry is a "shish kebab" and the more items of activity and responsibility he can add to his skewer, the less he worries about the absence of the main course.

The more closely the problem is observed the less inclined one is to call the fragmenting of the ministerial role a cause and the more convinced one is that it is a result—not, however, a result forced upon the minister by society or by the church but rather the result of the minister's own vocational instability. The epidemic ministerial sickness confronts us, in other words, not always with an occupational disease but sometimes with a shivered person. The probability, to state it more bluntly, is that the fragmentation of the minister is a result and a symptom of vocational ambivalence. If a minister neglects his pastoral-preaching-priestly duty, this may be merely a proof of laziness; but if he substitutes for that duty a host of other tasks which he gives priority and which require an equal amount of time and energy, this is an unintentional confession of vocational uncertainty. Ministers do not necessarily have a guilty feeling about this vocational indecision; they may, as we have noted, be totally unaware of the conflict between what they profess and what they practice. On the other hand, it is often the case that an avid search for proficiency in the secondary tasks reveals in the minister a submerged sense of guilt about his calling. The minister who is forever washing his hands in the minor activities of the church and in community affairs entirely detached from the church may argue that he is "getting things done" and is "applying religion to life," but the probability is that a guilty feeling about his vocation is driving him into increasingly frantic activity.

If the minister has serious doubts about his vocation—God's act—then qualms about his mission—his own act—are inevitable. That kind of anxiety is intolerable. The minister is usually too honest to dispel the problem by intellectualizing or rationalizing it—although he is not too honest to try—but he is human enough to let good works so absorb him that the problem—his doubt about his calling—seems to disappear. Anxiety is transformed into activity; and this activity, being fundamentally unfaithful to the minister's primary calling, in turn compounds his anxiety.

There is an even more critical danger from which, fortunately, God's grace or sheer human resiliency saves most ministers. Not to know who one is professionally is serious enough; not to know who one is personally is deadly. This peril confronts ministers with an assault which spares no man but to which the minister is especially vulnerable. The relationship between a man's *personage* (Paul Tournier's term) and his *person* is especially close in all professional men—as the title *professional* implies. (The actor is the only exception which comes to mind. The actor's problem is not to keep his life and his professional role closely identified but to keep them distinct.) For the Christian ministry far more than for any other profession, as Richard Siebeck put it, "it is the calling that creates the person." A man becomes a Christian minister when he responds to the imperious, specific, and particular claim of God. That claim demands not only the man's talent and his energy but simultaneously and inclusively his soul. To use some Pauline appellations, the minister is a slave of Jesus Christ, not his own, a prisoner, called to be an apostle, set apart for the gospel of God. This is what he is professionally and this is what he is personally. No doubt there are charlatans in the ministry as there are in all other professions; but in general it can be said that in the Christian ministry personage and person, profession and self, merge and become indistinguishable and inseparable. The Christian minister does not have a profession or pursue a profession; he *is* a profession.

It follows, then, that the minister's unfaithfulness to his calling—whether he neglect its duties in indolence or flee from those duties into exhilarating but peripheral activity—is suicidal. His life and his profession are Siamese twins with one blood flowing through two bodies which are so closely related that he cannot do violence to the one without doing harm to the other. And more specifically, the minister who, called to preach the gospel, has lost all enthusiasm for preaching and all awareness of the urgency of the gospel, may continue to wear to the people's view the ministerial face; but he will know and eventually the people will know that the face is a professional façade. The impersonation lingers; the person vanishes.

We return, then, to Paul's apostrophe and especially to the first words of it: "Woe to me if I do not preach the gospel." Consider what he might have said. He could have said, "Woe to the world if I do not preach the gospel." Knowing the impact that this greatest of the ancients had upon the world, we have to admit that this would not have been a presumptuous claim. He could have said, "Woe to the gospel if I do not preach it." Again, knowing Paul's part in keeping the flame of the gospel alive in a hostile world, we could not dismiss such a saying as arrogance. What he did say was *"Woe to me* if I do not preach the gospel." What did he mean?

Though Paul would not have put it in our terms, what he feared was that a refusal to preach the gospel entrusted to him would collapse the center of his being. The preaching of the gospel was his *raison d'être*. To him, a-man-called-Paul and the-preaching-of-the-gospel were not separate entities—one a man and the other what that man does—but were two descriptions of one thing. To be Paul was to be man-preaching-the-gospel; to cease preaching the gospel was to cease being Paul. If we could ask the Apostle what he meant by his "Woe to me," he would reply, "Woe to me because if I do not preach the gospel there will be no *me.*" His letter to the Philippians sharpens the focus of this thought: "For to me to live is Christ. . . ." His whole existence was engaged by Christ and the preaching of Christ; remove Christ from the formula and all the other factors would disappear. "Woe to me" was not the oath of a man who, doubtful of his resolution, swore a curse upon his possible disobedience. Rather it was his keen perception of the fact that Paul and the preaching of the gospel had either to be coalescent or nonexistent. T. R. Glover in a "by the way" in his *Paul of Tarsus* suggested this oneness of Paul and Paul's role: "Paul is the most autobiographical of writers, and the least. Every sentence is Paul, rather than Pauline, but chronology and quotation are work too slow for such a spirit."[3] This, then, was the identity: to be Paul was to preach the gospel; to preach the gospel was to be Paul.

The Scottish Baptist preacher and expositor, Alexander Maclaren, said that Paul "differs from us in the direct supernatural commission which was given to him, in the width of the sphere in which he had to work, and in the splendor of the gifts which were entrusted to his stewardship, he does not differ from us in the reality of the obligation which was laid upon him."[4] Out of a tradition which stressed the ministry of the laity Maclaren applied "the reality of the obligation" to every Christian's duty to preach the gospel. We must apply that obligation narrowly and specifically to the clergy. It is not "flesh and blood" that makes a minister but God's appointment, an appointment confirmed by the church and for most ministers an appointment including an order from God and the church to preach the gospel. Moreover, that order is not only explicit in the minister's appointment and in his ordination. It is implicit in the gospel: good news demands proclamation. W. H. Griffith Thomas in *The Work of the Ministry* calls our attention to the fact that Colossians I relates the ministry at once to Christ, to the gospel, and to the church—to Christ as the source, to the gospel as the message, and to the church as the sphere. All three impel the minister to proclaim God's good news to men: Christ by direct command, the gospel by its inherent urgency, and the church by its need.

It is therefore incorrect to speak of the minister *as* preacher as though preaching were a role to take up and put down. The minister *is* preacher, not *as*. Under the authority of Christ, the gospel, and the church he is made a preacher. If he accepts this appointment he cannot with impunity neglect it, slough it off, or substitute some other "good work" in its place. Unless he makes his peace with God and receives release or alternate service, refusal to preach the gospel in its purity and its power destroys him not only as a preacher but also as a man. This is the ministerial problem pushed to its depth. The problem is not that the world pushes in upon him with more demands than he can satisfy or that his schedule of study and meditation is canceled by his involvement in an activistic society. Rather the root of the problem is that the ultimacy and the totality of Christ's claim upon him is accepted with reservations; his belief in the uniqueness, universality, and finality of the gospel is shaky; and his confidence that God has made him peculiarly and indispensably the herald of the Promise is weak.

Why did Paul say to the Romans, "I am eager to preach the gospel to you also who are in Rome" (Rom. 1:15)? The words which surround this saying can easily mislead us by their closeness to this declaration. The preceding words, "I am under obligation both to Greeks and to barbarians, both to the wise and to the foolish" (Rom. 1:14), could be taken as Paul's confession that a deep indebtedness compels him to preach to the Romans. There is no question about the indebtedness or about Paul's awareness of it or about its compulsion. But this horizontal obligation, strong as it was, does not explain Paul's eagerness to tell Greeks and barbarians, the wise and the foolish, what he knew through Christ. The succeeding words, "For I am not ashamed of the gospel . . ." (Rom. 1:16), have been interpreted as evidence that Paul was tempted to be ashamed of the gospel and that by preaching it in the capital of the gentile world could prove to that world as well as to himself that he was guiltless of such shame. It is presumptuous to say that this simple denial is apologetic.

Undoubtedly behind Paul's preaching there were several powerful motivations, but we must look further if we are to discover that dynamic which made Paul an eager preacher of the gospel. We find the answer in the first words of his letter to the Romans: "Paul, a servant [a slave] of Jesus Christ . . ." (Rom. 1:1). This was a characteristic Pauline signature; this was his mark: he bore on his body and in his soul "the marks of Jesus"; he was possessed. It was a glad, voluntary slavery and he was gladly and voluntarily obedient to it. He was the freest and the most confident man of his time, and his freedom and confidence issued from his refusal to be "disobedient to the heavenly vision" and his resolve to "take every thought captive to obey Christ." Conviction followed action; he knew because he obeyed.

The Christian theory of knowing—which is similar to, but entirely separate from, the disputed James-Lange theory of emotion—is that Christian knowledge is the result of Christian obedience: "if any man's will is to do his will, he shall know whether the teaching is from God or whether I am speaking on my own authority" (John 7:17). As Robertson put it in one of his sermon titles, obedience is the organ of spiritual knowledge. Paul's confidence in Christ was in large part a result of the fact that he preached Christ in obedience to the will of Christ. He became what he was by doing what Christ had enjoined him to do.

We shall not in this later day recover the wholeness of the ministry unless ministers in obedience to Christ eagerly preach his urgent gospel. This is not, as some critics may say, a kind of autosuggestion. It is simply to say that we can know the truth that is in Christ only from within, only in total involvement, only in obedience to the will of Christ as it has been made known to us. Our food, too, like the Master's, is to do the will of him who sent us. And his will is that we "preach the word, be urgent in season and out of season, convince, rebuke, and exhort, be unfailing in patience and in teaching" (II Tim. 4:2).

Notes

Chapter 1   The Priority of the Spoken Word

1. Stopford, A. Brooke, ed., *Life and Letters of Frederick W. Robertson* (Boston: Ticknor and Fields, 1865), Vol. II, pp. 59–60.
2. *Ibid.,* Vol. I, p. 191.
3. *Ibid.,* Vol. II, pp. 59–60.
4. From St. Augustine, *On Christian Doctrine,* translated, with an introduction by D. W. Robertson, Jr. (New York: The Liberal Arts Press, Inc., 1958) Reprinted by permission of The Liberal Arts Press Division of The Bobbs-Merrill Company, Inc.

Chapter 2   The Urgency of Preaching

1. Stopford A. Brooke, ed., *Life and Letters of Frederick W. Robertson* (Boston: Ticknor and Fields, 1865), Vol. II, p. 88.
2. Richard S. Storrs, *Bernard of Clairvaux* (New York: Charles Scribner's Sons, 1912), p. 360.
3. Frederick Barton, compiler, *One Hundred Revival Sermons and Outlines* (New York: Harper & Brothers, 1906), p. 22.
4. Gaius Glenn Atkins, ed., *Master Sermons of the Nineteenth Century* (Chicago: Willett, Clark & Co., 1940), p. 100.
5. George A. Buttrick, *Sermons Preached in a University Church* (Nashville: Abingdon Press, 1959), p. 13.

6. Quoted by John D. Godsey, in *The Theology of Dietrich Bonhoeffer* (Philadelphia: The Westminster Press, 1960), p. 166.

7. James Black, *The Mystery of Preaching* (Westwood, N.J.: Fleming H. Revell Co., 1924), p. 26.

8. Herbert H. Farmer, *God and Men* (London: Nisbet & Co., Ltd., 1948), p. 147.

9. Herman Melville, *Moby Dick* (New York: The Modern Library, Random House, 1950), p. 225.

10. *Ibid.*, p. 567.

11. Horace Bushnell, *Christian Nurture* (New Haven: Yale University Press, 1947), p. 4.

12. Kenneth Hamilton, *The Protestant Way* (Fair Lawn, N.J.: Essential Books, Inc., 1956), p. 110.

13. *The Interpreter's Bible* (New York and Nashville: Abingdon Press, 1952), Vol. VIII, p. 223.

Chapter 3   The Meaning of Relevant Preaching

1. Dietrich Ritschl, *A Theology of Proclamation* (Richmond, Va.: John Knox Press, 1960), p. 8.

2. David Bryn-Jones, *God's Grace and Man's Condition* (Rutland, Vt.: Charles E. Tuttle Co., 1954), pp. 8–9.

3. George A. Buttrick, *Sermons Preached in a University Church* (Nashville: Abingdon Press, 1959), p. 7.

4. John Ruskin, *Sesame and Lilies* (New York: F. M. Lupton Co., 1871), p. 77.

5. Maurice Maeterlinck, *The Life of the Bee* (New York: Dodd, Mead and Co., 1902), pp. 30–31.

6. Quoted by Harry Emerson Fosdick, in *Living under Tension* (New York: Harper & Brothers, 1941), p. 193.

7. Frederick Keller Stamm, ed., *The Best of Charles E. Jefferson* (New York: Thomas Y. Crowell, 1960), p. 205.

8. J. H. Jowett, *Apostolic Optimism* (London: A. C. Armstrong and Son, 1902), pp. 267–68.

9. E. L. Magoon, ed., *Sermons of the Rev. C. H. Spurgeon* (Chicago: Sheldon, Blakeman and Co., 1857), p. xix.

Chapter 4   Recovering the Preacher's Identity

1. *Preaching in These Times* (New York: Charles Scribner's Sons, 1940), p. 55. (The Lyman Beecher Lectures on Preaching in 1940 were given by six lecturers.)

2. Franklin Hamlin Littell, *From State Church to Pluralism* (Chicago: Aldine Publishing Co., 1962), pp. 126–27.

3. T. R. Glover, *Paul of Tarsus* (New York: George H. Doran Co., 1925), p. 27.

4. Alexander Maclaren, *Expositions of Holy Scripture* (London: Hodder & Stoughton, 1904–1910, Vol. 18, p. 132.

Format by Anne Hallowell
Set in Linotype Granjon
Composed by York Composition Company, Inc.
Printed and bound by The Haddon Craftsmen, Inc.
HARPER & ROW, PUBLISHERS, INCORPORATED

251
H34